AF252171

Political Economy of Agricultural Trade-Related Policies in China

Series on Contemporary China   (ISSN: 1793-0847)

Series Editors: Joseph Fewsmith *(Boston University)*
Zheng Yong-Nian *(East Asian Institute, National University of Singapore)*

This series showcases the most significant and lasting contributions to scholarship in the studies of China's politics, society, and culture — whether for general readers or specialists. Each of the volumes is a quality work by a leading scholar or scholars in the field and may take the form of a research monograph, a multi-author edited volume, a conference proceeding, a textbook, or an annual review, among others. While the focus is on China, the series does not lose sight of the interplay of other regional and global forces and their influence and impact on China.

Series on Contemporary China – Vol. 47

Political Economy of Agricultural Trade-Related Policies in China

Wenshou Yan

Zhongnan University of Economics and Law, China

NEW JERSEY · LONDON · SINGAPORE · BEIJING · SHANGHAI · HONG KONG · TAIPEI · CHENNAI · TOKYO

Published by

World Scientific Publishing Co. Pte. Ltd.

5 Toh Tuck Link, Singapore 596224

USA office: 27 Warren Street, Suite 401-402, Hackensack, NJ 07601

UK office: 57 Shelton Street, Covent Garden, London WC2H 9HE

Library of Congress Cataloging-in-Publication Data

Names: Yan, Wenshou, author.

Title: Political economy of agricultural trade-related policies in China /
 Wenshou Yan, Zhongnan University of Economics and Law, China.

Description: USA : World Scientific, 2020. | Series: Series on contemporary China, 1793-0847 ; 47 |
 Includes bibliographical references.

Identifiers: LCCN 2020020089 | ISBN 9789811218897 (hardcover) | ISBN 9789811218903 (ebook) |
 ISBN 9789811218910 (ebook other)

Subjects: LCSH: Produce trade--Government policy--China. |
 Agricultural prices--Government policy--China. | Farm produce--Storage--China. |
 China--Commercial policy. | China--Commerce.

Classification: LCC HD9016.C62 Y3236 2020 | DDC 382.4/10951--dc23

LC record available at https://lccn.loc.gov/2020020089

British Library Cataloguing-in-Publication Data

A catalogue record for this book is available from the British Library.

For any available supplementary material, please visit
https://www.worldscientific.com/worldscibooks/10.1142/11786#t=suppl

Desk Editors: Aanand Jayaraman/Lixi Dong

Typeset by Stallion Press
Email: enquiries@stallionpress.com

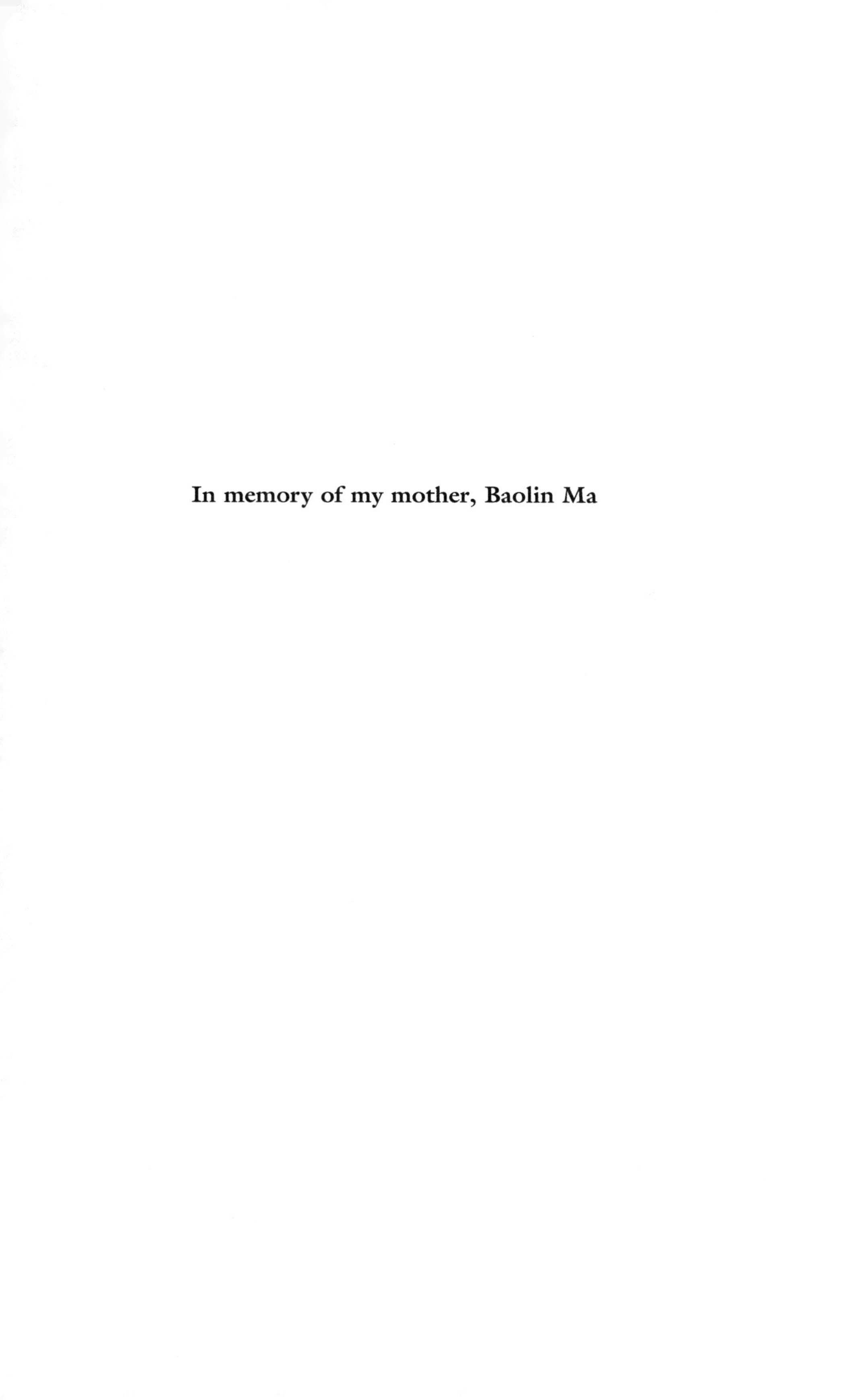

In memory of my mother, Baolin Ma

Preface

This book seeks to understand the simultaneous economic and political contributors to China's changing agricultural protection levels and the central government's choice of policy instruments to tax or assist farmers. It begins in Chapter 2 by theoretically exploring the motivations behind agricultural trade-related support policies by extending the two-sector specific factors production model to three sectors, to make it more relevant for a one-party state such as China. The review suggests that the switch from taxing to subsidizing the agricultural sector depends not only on changes in the economy's structure but, more critically, on the underlying political support from heterogeneous interest groups in the course of economic development. The equilibrium agricultural protection level is determined by equating the marginal political returns from supporting farmers to marginal political costs from opposing groups (including manufacturers).

Chapter 3 tests that theory empirically, using panel data on agricultural distortions for the period 1981–2010 from Anderson and Nelgen (2013). When using the relative rate of assistance as the agricultural protection indicator, the results are robust. The study concludes that (1) arable land per capita, the proportion of the workforce in the agricultural sector, and the self-sufficiency ratio are more significant in China than elsewhere, and (2) inequality is more significant than poverty in contributing to the changes in China's agricultural trade-related policies.

Around that long-running trend in the level of assistance to the farm sector are considerable fluctuations in support from year to year, not least because of fluctuations in international prices of agricultural products. Chapter 4 seeks to explain the Chinese government's responses to world market price fluctuations. It develops a theoretical model of trade policy incorporating loss aversion and reference dependence. Like Freund and Özden (2008), this chapter (unlike Chapter 5) assumes only trade policy instruments are available to the government, but it goes beyond their model by adding a spatial dimension to interest group politics. The model suggests that (1) politically sensitive products receive more trade protection; (2) the government's changing trade distortions insulate the domestic market from international price fluctuations by setting trade protection lower (higher) when the world price is higher (lower) than a targeted domestic reference price; and (3) variations in market intervention help producers at the expense of consumers in periods when the international price is well below trend, and help consumers at the expense of producers in high-price periods. These predictions from theory are shown to still hold when the model is extended to a large country case involving terms of trade effects. The model is tested empirically and found to offer a plausible explanation for the puzzling changes in cotton protection in China.

In practice, the government does have other instruments besides trade restrictions to alter domestic producer and consumer prices in the face of fluctuating international prices. Chapter 5 explores the role that public storage policy can play in contributing to the government's objective of stabilizing the domestic market price of farm products. The political economy theory developed in Chapter 4 is extended to incorporate domestic storage, so as to explore government motivations in the context of border and domestic policy coordination. Domestic storage policy can add to price stabilization in the presence of trade policies, and can reinforce a price-insulating trade policy by increasing the country's market power. However, the effects of these two price stabilization instruments on the international market price are in opposite directions. The effect of storage on the world market is then tested, again using China cotton as a case study. The VAR econometrics reveals that in the case of cotton during 2011–2014, China as a large player in the global market was able to stabilize to a non-trivial extent the international price of cotton by altering its public stockpile.

The final chapter of the book draws out implications for policy-makers in China and elsewhere. One is that the Chinese government should not apply trade distortions since they reduce resource allocation efficiency, social welfare, and consumer utility. Another is that domestic public storage policy, rather than trade distortions, could be an effective way to achieve domestic political targets. If managed well enough, storage could be less distortive of world agricultural markets than trade policy, but if poorly managed, it could add to the disruptions that trade policies bring to those markets.

About the Author

 **Wenshou Yan** is an Assistant Professor at the School of Business Administration at Zhongnan University of Economics and Law. He obtained both his Bachelor's (2009) and Master's (2012) degrees in Finance from Northwest A&F University. He earned his Ph.D. degree in Economics from the University of Adelaide in December 2016, where he was awarded the honor of "Dean's Commendation for Doctoral Thesis Excellence". His principal research interests are in the fields of international trade theory and policy, new political economy, agricultural development, and the interface between them. He joined Zhongnan University of Economics and Law at the beginning of 2017, and he began supervising master's students from September 2018. He has published several papers in peer-reviewed journals such as *Economic Modelling*, *Australian Journal of Agricultural and Resource Economics*, *Manchester School*, *Scottish Journal of Political Economy*, *Asian-Pacific Economic Literature*, and *China Agricultural Economic Review*.

Acknowledgments

First and foremost, I would like to sincerely thank my principal supervisor Professor Kym Anderson for his time, generous supervision, and insightful advice during the past 4 years at the University of Adelaide. The joy, enthusiasm, and diligence he has for his research were contagious and motivational for me. Without his guidance and assistance, this book could not have been completed.

My appreciation also goes to my co-supervisors, Dr. Florian Ploeckl, Dr. Nicholas Sim, and Dr. Tatyana Chesnokova. They provided valuable comments and advice to enable me to complete this book.

I also benefited from the courses and workshops taught by Professor Kym Anderson, Dr. Tatyana Chesnokova, Dr. Terence Cheng, Dr. Firmin Doko Tchatoka, Dr. Dmitriy Kvasov, Professor Paul Pezanis-Christou, Professor Richard Pomfret, Dr. Nicholas Sim, and Dr. Jacob Wong. I am thankful also to the professional staff at the School of Economics who helped in a number of ways. Financial support from the China Scholarship Council is gratefully acknowledged as well.

I also express my thanks to my friends, especially Di, Kai, Xiaobo, Faqin, Hang, Jiang, Dou, Lin, Qin, Xue, Kaixing, Ye, Wenxi, Wenxiao, and Lingyu, for caring and supporting me.

Finally, I wish to thank my wife Xi Yang for her support and encouragement, and my baby Ruichen Yan, who gives me the greatest incentive to enjoy life. I also thank my family members and Xi's family members for their endless love, understanding, and unconditional support, which could not be enumerated here one by one.

With my deepest appreciation to all.

Contents

List of Figures

List of Tables

List of Abbreviations

CIF	Cost, Insurance, and Freight
FE	Fixed Effect
FEVD	Forecast Error Variance Decompositions
GDP	Gross Domestic Product
G–H	Grossman and Helpman
H–O	Heckscher–Ohlin
H–T	Harris–Todaro
IFPRI	International Food Policy Research Institute
IRF	Impulse Response Function
J–B	Jarque–Bera
NCCA	National Cotton Council of America
NRA	Nominal Rate of Assistance
OECD	Organisation for Economic Co-operation and Development
PPP	Purchasing Power Parity
RMB	Renminbi
ROW	Rest of the World
RRA	Relative Rate of Assistance
SSD	Sliding Scale Duty
SUR	Stock-to-Use Ratio

TRQ	Tariff Rate Quota
USDA	United States Department of Agriculture
VAR	Vector Auto-Regression
VMPL	Value of Marginal Product of Labor
WTO	World Trade Organization
XPCC	Xinjiang Production and Construction Corporation

Introduction

1.1 Background

China's fast-growing economy in the past 35 years has benefited hugely from policy reforms and opening to the world. China became the second-largest economy in the world in 2010, and has been working toward the top spot in the coming years. China's dramatic growth has lifted hundreds of millions of people out of poverty and sharply increased urbanization.

Prior to 2000, China had in place anti-agricultural policies aimed at keeping food and fiber prices for consumers lower than those in the international market during that period. But after 2000, the Chinese government turned to pro-agricultural and trade policies, which slowed the relative decline of the agricultural sector. These distortionary policies are harmful to resource allocation efficiency, social welfare, and long-run economic growth. One interesting question is as follows: Why has the Chinese government chosen to distort agricultural incentives in these differing ways through time?

The question is worth exploring for two reasons. First, as emphasized by Nobel Laureate G. Stigler (1975, p. ix), "Until we understand why your society adopts its policies, we will be poorly equipped to give useful advice on how to change these policies." In other words, understanding policy formation is a prerequisite for advocating policy reform and then implementing new policies. This understanding is necessary for advancing the economy and improving the social welfare of China. Second, the expanding role of China in the world market has attracted lot of attention from other countries and non-government organizations. China's agricultural trade-related policies have a critical effect on importers and exporters, and the world agricultural market. As emphasized by Anderson and Hayami (1986:1), "Such an understanding is also required for forecasting trends in production, consumption, and trade for growing economies." Such forecasts are beneficial to production determination, consumption choice, and agricultural and trade policy reform for other countries, as well as for China.

Numerous countries have begun to reform their agricultural and trade policies in the past 30 years, leading to the liberalization of global agricultural trade. Unfortunately, the process has not been as fast as in non-farm sectors, with distortions in agricultural and trade markets persisting in both developing and developed countries (Anderson, 2009). Not only do these distortionary policies waste resources and exacerbate inequality and poverty but they also hinder progress in multilateral trade negotiations (Anderson, 2010).

China's Nominal Rate of Assistance[1] to farmers was minus 40% in 1986–1988, but by 2010–2012 it had increased to 18% for tradable products (Anderson and Strutt, 2014). This changing pattern of distortions to incentives (detailed in Section 2 of Chapter 2) follows a similar long-term policy trajectory of developed countries and copies the experiences of neighboring countries such as Japan and South Korea (Anderson and Hayami, 1986).

What governments do in response to short-term fluctuations in world market prices also matters. During the past half-century,

---

[1]The Nominal Rate of Assistance (NRA) is defined as the percent by which gross returns to farmers have been raised above international levels by government policies (Anderson *et al.*, 2008).

international agricultural markets have experienced three price spikes: two upward price spike periods (1973–1974 and 2007–2008) and a downward spike period (1984–1986). Domestic market prices broadly follow international market prices in numerous low- and middle-income countries, where the consumption-weighted local price increased by 19%, 19%, and 29% for rice, wheat, and maize, respectively, in 2007–2008 (Dawe *et al.*, 2015). In the face of international price fluctuations, the Chinese government has adopted numerous policies in the past to stabilize domestic agricultural markets, including altering border trade restrictions and volumes in national public storage.

This book first investigates the theoretical motivations of China's agricultural trade-related policies in the long term. That theory is empirically tested to explore the different determinants of distortionary policies between China and the rest of the world (ROW). In the context of recent world agricultural price spikes, Chapter 4 explores incentives for the government to alter trade restrictions in the short term. Then, Chapter 5 focuses on adding public storage to the policy options, and examines the effects of China's cotton stock changes.

1.2 Literature Review

1.2.1 *Determinants of long-term trends in distortion policies*

The literature on what determines agricultural and trade protection in the long term is divided into two branches: comparative advantage theory and political economy determination theory. Agricultural protection is more likely to increase in the course of economic development of a country if its agricultural comparative advantage is declining. Recent empirical tests indicate that the protection level is positively related to real GDP per capita, but negatively related to arable land per capita (Anderson, 2009). Previous tests include Anderson and Hayami (1986) and Krueger (1992). During the 1980s and 1990s, the literature summarized three types of patterns: the "development pattern", the "anti-trade pattern", and the "anti-comparative advantage pattern" (Swinnen, 2010b). From the individual level, social status, relative income, values, and a preference for trade policies are investigated by Melgar *et al.* (2013), who find that skilled laborers are more likely to support free trade than unskilled laborers.

Numerous other traditional political models, including regulation theory (Stigler, 1971), group pressure theory (Becker, 1983, 1985), policy preference function (Rausser and Freebairn, 1974), political support function (Hillman, 1982), political preference function (Bullock, 1994), and conservative social welfare function (Corden, 1997), help to explain why governments implement inefficient policies in different sectors. Grossman and Helpman (1994) develop a money contribution model which provides the effective micro-foundation for trade protection policy analysis. In parallel with the group money contribution model, the tariff formation function model (Findlay and Wellisz, 1982), the campaign contribution model (Magee *et al.*, 1989), the political support model (Rodrick, 1995), and the median voter model (Mayer, 1984) have also been developed to analyze agricultural policy formation.

In the context of dynamic behavior, many studies are devoted to agent's preferences, displaying behavioral characteristics such as loss aversion and reference dependence (Freund and Özden, 2008; Tovar, 2009).

1.2.2 *Short-term trade restrictiveness and world price fluctuations*

During periods of world price fluctuations, including upward and downward spike periods, many countries alter their export- or import-restrictive instruments to reduce price instability by insulating the domestic market from the international market. Those countries importing food and agricultural products are afraid that exporting countries will suddenly limit their exports. The alternative changes of import and export restrictions are frequently levied in response to food security concerns or media hype over agriculture.

Articles documenting the effects of agricultural trade insulation policies during food price spike periods include Abbott (2011), Anderson (2013), Ivanic and Martin (2014), and Thennakoon and Anderson (2015). Anderson and Nelgen (2012b) find that governments adjust trade policies in response to upward or downward price spikes by the same magnitude, which implies that a prevention of downward price spikes is likely to arise from a concern for producer welfare. The unilateral action by exporting countries' policies[2] gives rise to a "multiplier effect" by imposing export restrictions (subsidies) when a shock in the world food market drives up (down) the international price (Giordani *et al.*, 2016).

During world price fluctuation periods, importers' and exporters' combined actions have accentuated the upward or downward spikes in the international market price following a price shock (Anderson and Nelgen, 2012b; Thennakoon and Anderson, 2015). For a non-democratic, fast-growing economy such as China, what are the government's incentives for altering trade restrictiveness in the short run in such a price spike context? One aim of this book is to improve our understanding of how the Chinese government responds to world price fluctuations.

1.2.3 *Domestic public storage policy and price stabilization*

Based on information from 81 countries, 68 of them used trade policy measures during the 2007–2008 food crisis period (Demeke *et al.*, 2009). The collective impact of their trade insulation policy was to further raise the international price (Anderson *et al.*, 2014). According to previous research, national public storage is another way to cushion the local market price. Wright and Williams (1988) argue that to achieve price stabilization the focus should be on stabilizing

---

[2] The multiplier effect of trade policies is mainly driven by large countries, but when many small countries also respond, their collective behavior will add to the aggravation of the world market price.

quantities, not prices. Stocks accumulate when supply is large, and storage is released for consumption in times of scarcity. However, the domestic price is highly sensitive when there is a low level of storage of agricultural products globally. Could an optimal combination of national storage and trade policies stabilize domestic food prices? This is possible because, without intervention, price dynamics are driven by productive domestic shocks and international prices (Gouel and Jean, 2015). However, one of the drawbacks of trade policies is that it may aggravate high world price episodes in a small open economy. Thus, the role of domestic public storage on the world market price is rarely seen, and the effect is unclear in a large country.

1.3 Research Questions

China is the third-largest country in the world in area, and the most populous. It has experienced dramatic economic growth during the past 35 years after opening to the world in 1978, yet it continues to be ruled by just one political party. Given that context, this book addresses two key questions. First, what determines the government's agricultural trade-related policy formation in the long term, and how do those determinants differ from ones affecting trade and agricultural policymaking in countries that are not subject to one-party rule? Second, how does the government of China respond to short-term fluctuations in international prices of farm products, and again how does that differ from the reactions of governments in other countries? The latter question is important because both producers and consumers are sensitive to changes in food prices, and spikes in those prices are closely related to political unrest (Arezki and Bruckner, 2011; Bellemare, 2014). The Chinese government has sought to stabilize domestic agricultural markets not only by insulating them from international price movements but also by altering domestic public stocks. In the case of cotton, for example, China raised its stocks to more than 55% of the world's total production in 2014. The final key question addressed in this book is as follows: What are the effects of China's cotton storage program on the international market for cotton?

1.4 Structure of the Book

The agricultural sector provides an ideal experiment for us to explore government behavior. Chapter 2 presents a theory of the simultaneous economic and political driving forces affecting China's evolving agricultural protection levels. The author explores the motivations and incentives for adopting Chinese agricultural trade-related policies by extending to three sectors the specific factor model of a traditional dual economy. The results indicate that the switching from taxing to subsidizing of the agricultural sector depends not only on the changing economic structure but more critically also on the underlying political support from heterogeneous interest groups that are evolving in the course of economic development in a one-party-ruled developing country.

Chapter 3 examines the political forces behind changing agricultural protection levels during 1981–2010 for China as compared with other countries. Using an econometric regression model, the author finds that arable land per capita, the proportion of the work force in the agricultural sector, and the self-sufficiency ratio have stronger effects on agricultural protection in China than elsewhere, and inequality plays a larger role than poverty in contributing to the variation across farm industries in China's agricultural protection levels.

In contrast to the long-term analysis in Chapters 2 and 3, Chapter 4 focuses on how the Chinese government responds to short-term spikes in international prices of farm products. A theoretical model of trade policy is developed to incorporate loss aversion and reference dependence along the lines of Freund and Özden (2008) but modified for a non-democratic country characterized with spatial dimensions of interest group politics. The results show that politically sensitive products receive greater trade protection, that trade distortions are altered to insulate the domestic market from international price spikes, and that the variations in trade distortion balance domestic income redistribution between producers and consumers in the short term irrespective of politically sensitive groups. This chapter also shows that the model can explain the cotton protection policy in China.

The Chinese government also has varied public storage of farm products in an attempt to stabilize the domestic market price in the face of fluctuating international prices. In Chapter 5, the political economy theory is extended to incorporate domestic storage to explore government motivations behind coordinating its border and domestic policies. The theoretical political economy model predicts that domestic storage policy could not only contribute to price stabilization but also influence the international price. However, the effects of the two instruments on the Nash equilibrium international market price are in opposite directions. That is, these results indicate that domestic public storage policy has a price stabilization effect not only on the domestic market but also on the international market price.

The author's empirical simulation in Chapter 5 estimates the effects of national storage, again using China cotton as a case study, on the world cotton market between 2011 and 2014. By adopting a dynamic simulation method using counterfactual data, the results indicate that the sharp increase of China cotton storage contributed to the rebound of world cotton price from the highest spike level in 2010 to a more normal price level. The dynamic mechanism is more complicated than static partial equilibrium model predictions. The mechanism is that the selling of China's cotton stocks depresses world cotton production and cotton storage by the ROW, resulting in an increase of the world cotton market price and a decline in global cotton consumption.

Chapter 6 draws out some policy implications related to how to reform government policies, and how to choose between trade interventions and domestic public storage policy.

Determinants of Agricultural Protection Trends in China: Theory

2.1 Introduction

One of the puzzles in economics is why governments adopt inefficient and suboptimal public policies. The agricultural sector provides an ideal experiment to explore government behavior. Since the establishment of the People's Republic of China, the Chinese government has been distorting the agricultural sector using domestic and trade policies. The changes in the extent of those distortions to domestic prices are shown in Fig. 2.1 in terms of Nominal Rates of Assistance (NRA), where the NRA is defined as the proportional increase in the gross value of production due to government policies. If that assistance is just in the form of an import restriction that raises the domestic price above the international price at the country's border, it is simply expressed as $NRA = \frac{(P_t - P_t^*)}{(P_t^*)}$ where P_t is the domestic price and P_t^* is the border price at time t. If the NRA is higher (lower) than zero, it means the Chinese government subsidizes (taxes) the agricultural sector.

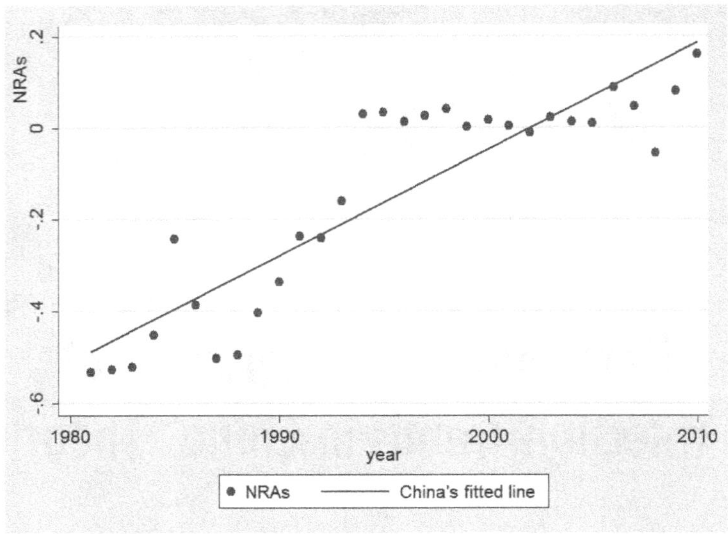

Fig. 2.1 China's changing agricultural protection levels during 1981–2010.
Source: Anderson and Nelgen (2013).

China launched myriad policy reforms from the late 1970s, including land reform and opening to the world. Even so, up to the mid-1990s, the government was still directly or indirectly discouraging the agricultural sector relative to the industry sector, thereby assisting net buyers of farm products and encouraging industrial development. By contrast, the Chinese government has been executing pro-agricultural and pro-poor agricultural trade-related policies from 2004 after the release of the "first file of the central government". That is, the government transitioned from taxing to subsiding agriculture relative to manufacturing over the decade 1995–2004, and the agricultural protection level has sharply increased since then (Table 2.1).

The main purpose of this chapter is to explore the determinants of China's agricultural protection levels over the past 35 years. A better understanding of the reasons for China's policy choices is important because of the large and increasing role of China in the world market for farm products. Having a better understanding of the current agricultural policies of China will also help analysts project China's future agricultural policies and their impact on food supply and demand.

Table 2.1 Agricultural protection levels in China, 1981–2014.

	1981–1984	1985–1989	1990–1994	1995–1999	2000–2004	2005–2009	2010–2012
NRA ag. tradable	−45	−36	−14	7	6	6	18
NRA non-ag.	42	28	25	10	5	4	4
RRA	−61	−50	−31	−3	1	2	14

Notes: $\text{RRA} = \left[\dfrac{1+\text{NRA}_{ag^t}}{1+\text{NRA}_{nonag^t}} - 1 \right]$ refers to the relative rate of assistance to agriculture sector, and NRA_{ag^t} and NRA_{nonag^t} are the percentage NRAs for the tradable parts of the agricultural and non-agricultural sectors.

Source: Anderson and Strutt (2014).

To model the political economy of China's farm policies, we build on the traditional specific-factor model developed by Jones (1971).[1] The structure of China's economy in the course of its economic development does not simply track the dual economy predicted by Lewis (1954). China's township and village enterprises, and some small processing firms began to emerge after 1979 and became highly developed after the mid-1990s. In the context of township and village enterprises and processing firms, a tripartite economic structure has formed (Li, 1994). Hence, a three-sector model is more applicable for analyzing income distributional effects of trade-related policies and thereby China's political economy of policymaking. The political model developed in Section 2.3, following Swinnen (1994), is based on relaxed ownership assumptions of different productive factors. Results from that model are then inputs into a partial equilibrium model of the political market for policies (drawing on Anderson, 1992) used in Section 2.4 to explain changing agricultural protection levels.[2] The final section concludes this chapter and draws some policy implications.

---

[1] The specific factor model is the standard three-factor, two-goods trade model used for short-run analysis. One factor is freely mobile between the two sectors, and the other two factors are fixed in each sector.

[2] Even though the Chinese government views the organized lobbying groups as threats to her political power, interest groups nonetheless exist in China. When

2.2 Literature Review

Related literature tracing back to the 1960s has found that agricultural protection is more likely to increase as a country develops and as agricultural comparative advantage declines (Anderson and Hayami, 1986; Krueger, 1992; Anderson, 2009).[3] During the 1980s and 1990s, the earlier literature identified three patterns: the "development pattern", the "anti-trade pattern", and the "anti-comparative advantage pattern" (Swinnen, 2010b).

As well as traditional economic factors having an effect on trade distortions, political factors also have attracted more attention by researchers in recent years. The empirical literature includes Olper (2007) who tests the effects of land ownership inequality and government ideology on agricultural protection levels and finds that protection is decreasing in land inequality and that left-wing governments are more likely to support the agricultural sector in more unequal societies. Lobby group modeling is also tested using data from the United States' agricultural sector (Gawande and Hoekman, 2006), and it too finds that lobby groups influence agricultural protection levels.

The above models are trying to explain what contributes to the formation of agricultural protection policies using economic and political factors in democratic countries. Can we apply these models to Chinese policy analysis? In the case of China, Huang *et al.* (2015) analyze the government's agricultural and food policies from a short-term perspective. They review the political structure of the policy-making process and how the government could effectively use policies in response to short-term world price spikes. Concerning long-term trend analysis, Branstettera and Feenstra (2002) develop a theoretical model based on the Grossman and Helpman model (1994) and empirically test the structural parameters using province-level data on

---

making public policies, the government would consider the prospective gains or losses for different types of interest groups from any changes to public policies.

[3] In a study in which global agricultural protection levels have been calculated (Anderson *et al.*, 2009, 2013), the world is divided into five regions: the developing countries of Asia, Africa, and Latin America, plus Europe's transition economies and advanced economies.

foreign direct investment and trade flows in China. The results indicate that the one-party government seeks to maximize state-owned enterprises' profits rather than the welfare of consumers. Sheng (2006) econometrically tests the simultaneous determinants of China trade policy using time series and cross-section data, and concludes that party ideology, government preferences, and national interests are the most important determinants of policy-making in China.

2.3 Income Distribution Model

2.3.1 *Why extend to a three-sector model?*

In this section, the traditional two-sector specific-factors model of Jones (1971), Mayer (1974), and Mussa (1974) is extended to three sectors. This extension is desirable because in China, unskilled labor intensive township and village enterprises and processing firms play a critical role in utilizing farm labor in rural areas. Unskilled laborers also work in urban manufacturing industries, and more so since the relaxing of the *Hukou* system. There are still many under-employed laborers in rural China (Zhang *et al.*, 2011), where wage income has become the main source of farm household income in some regions. If farmers are slow to adjust their competitiveness by obtaining off-farm employment, the gap between farm and non-farm household income will increase (Anderson and Strutt, 2014). The rate of labor absorption in the formal sector and of labor transfers from the agricultural sector to a formal sector are slowest for the least skilled workers.

2.3.2 *Model assumptions*

We assume that the economy has farm and non-farm communities.[4] The non- farm sector consists of a rural processing sector and an urban manufacturing sector. The structure of the economy is illustrated in

---

[4] Different terminologies are used to name the two sectors, for instance, formal vs informal, modern vs traditional, and industrial vs agricultural (Gollin, 2014). The author simply refers to farm and non-farm sectors.

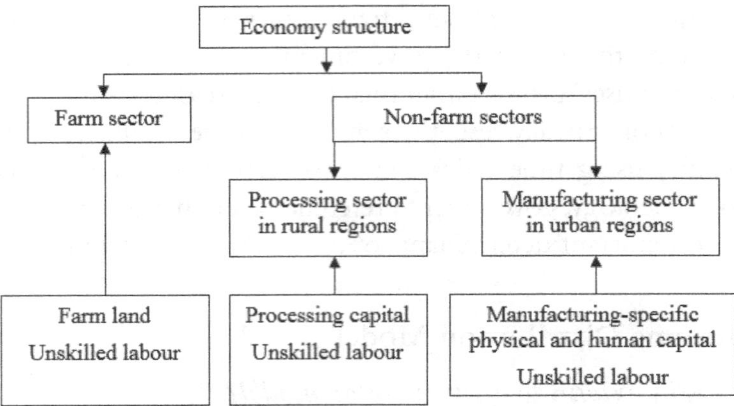

Fig. 2.2   Modeled structure of the economy.

Fig. 2.2. The three sub-sectors produce three types of final tradable commodities with constant returns to scale. Labor and capital are inputs used to produce the final goods, and each function is of a linear and homogeneous form exhibiting positive and declining marginal products for each factor. Agricultural land and unskilled labor are required to produce the agricultural product, and sector-specific physical capital and unskilled labor are used to process primary products in rural areas. To produce manufactured goods, sector-specific physical and human capital (i.e., skilled labor) and unskilled labor are needed, and skilled labor is part of the (human plus physical) stock of sector-specific capital employed in the urban manufacturing sector. The production functions are as follows for the farm sector, processing sector, and manufacturing sector:

Farm sector: $X_F = f(L_F, \overline{K_F})$
Rural processing sector: $X_P = f(L_P, \overline{K_P})$
Urban manufacturing sector: $X_M = f(L_M, \overline{K_M})$

The theoretical model in this chapter is not a long-term model as per the Heckscher–Ohlin model (H–O model). It is natural to consider capital as fixed in its sectoral usage in the short-to-medium term that is the timeframe typically used for policy reform decisions. However, we assume unskilled laborers are mobile between the three sectors. We further assume that the prices of the three sets of final tradable goods are given by the world price adjusted by the Chinese government's policies (the small country assumption).

2.3.3 *Three-sector general equilibrium assuming no trade distortions*

In a perfectly competitive factor market, each factor gets the value of its marginal product. Since the homogeneous unskilled laborers are mobile between rural and urban regions, and between farm and processing sectors within the rural area, there is a common wage w_r. The unskilled laborers get a higher wage rate w_u (the unionized minimum wage) if employed in the urban area, and a zero wage if unemployed, such that the weighted average unskilled wage in the urban area wage rate equals the wage in rural regions. The returns to specific factors are denoted by r_F, r_p, and r_M in the farm sector, processing sector, and manufacturing sector, respectively.[5] Figure 2.3 illustrates the three-sector specific-factor model. The horizontal line represents the total amount of unskilled labor in the economy, and the vertical lines indicate the wage rate for the unskilled laborers. VMPL($\cdot$)s stand for the value of marginal product of unskilled laborers in the agricultural sector, manufacturing sector, and non-farm sector, respectively. Completing the model requires linking the farm, processing, and manufacturing sectors together by establishing a common wage w_r at point B between the farm and processing sectors. w_u is the minimum wage rate in urban cities. The employment in the farm sector is indicated from left to right (OM). Because land is fixed in the farm sector and we assume that the agricultural price is fixed, as more labor is employed in the farm sector, the value of unskilled labor's marginal product declines as represented by the downward-sloping line. The value of marginal product of unskilled labor in the manufacturing

---

[5] Skilled laborers in the manufacturing sector are captured as the human capital component that contributes to the marginal product of total capital in the manufacturing sector. Therefore, skilled laborers in effect get the same rate of return (rM) as physical capital.

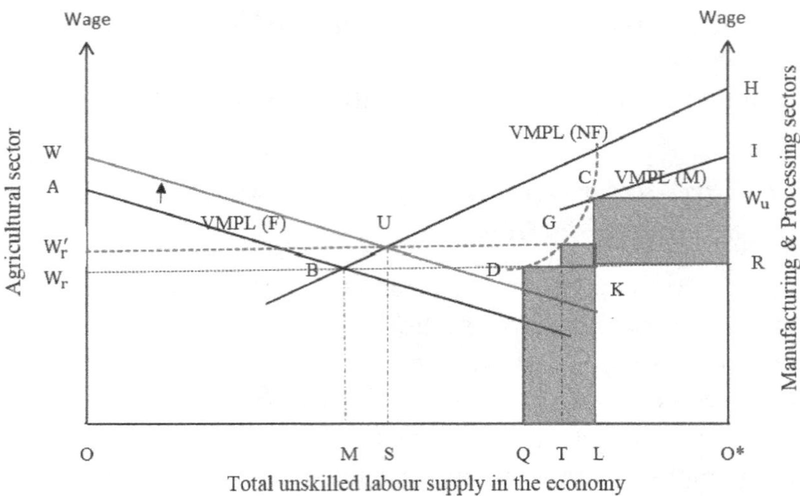

Fig. 2.3   Illustration of the model's market equilibrium.

sector (IC) and the non-farm sector (HB) could be drawn at a diminishing rate, respectively. The demand for labor in the manufacturing sector is represented by the VMPL(M) schedule which is drawn from right to left ($O*L$). The labor needed in processing sector is between the point M and point Q. The distance QL is the unemployment of unskilled labors in urban cities. Land earns the area ABw_r. Capital owners and skilled laborers in the manufacturing sector get the aggregate return indicated by the area ICw_u.

2.3.4 *Income redistribution effects of changing agricultural trade distortions*

The above three-sector specific-factors model is now used to analyze income redistribution effects of changing agricultural trade restrictiveness. The following symbols will be used to formalize the model:

a_{Ki}: Amount of capital required to produce 1 unit of output in the ith sector, and $i = F, P, M$;

a_{Li}: Unskilled labor–output ratio in the ith sector, and $i = F, P, M$;

P_i: Exogenous given price of commodity i relative to the manufactured good (normalized to 1), and $i = F, P$;

X_i: Level of output in the ith sector, and $i = F, P, M$;

w_r: Wage rate of the unskilled laborers in the rural area (in both the farm sector and processing sectors);

w_u: Wage rate in the manufacturing sector in the urban area;

r_i: Return to specific capital in the ith sector, and $i = F, P, M$;

K_i: Capital endowment in the ith sector, and $i = F, P, M$;

L: Unskilled labor endowment;

L_u: Unskilled labor unemployment in the urban area;

L_i: Unskilled labor allocation in ith sector, and $i = F, P, M$;

$\wedge$: Proportional change of factors;

θ_{Li}: Distributive share of unskilled labor in the ith sector, and $i = F, P, M$;

λ_{Li}: Fraction of the labor force in the ith sector, and $i = F, P, M$;

v: Employment rate of unskilled labor in the urban area.

With perfectly competitive commodity markets, the zero-profit conditions are:

$$a_{LF}\, w_r + a_{KF}\, r_F = P_r \tag{1}$$

$$a_{LP}\, w_r + a_{KP}\, r_P = P_P \tag{2}$$

$$a_{LM}\, w_u + a_{KM}\, r_M = 1 \tag{3}$$

The above three equations state that the unit cost of production of each good must be equal to its domestic price in equilibrium. The full-employment conditions of the four factors of production could be illustrated as follows:

$$a_{KF}\, X_F = K_F \tag{4}$$

$$a_{KP}\, X_P = K_P \tag{5}$$

$$a_{KM}\, X_M = K_M \tag{6}$$

$$a_{LF}\, X_F + a_{LP}\, X_P + a_{LM}\, X_M + L_u = L \tag{7}$$

The Harris–Todaro (1970) type unemployment (H–Y type hereafter) is included in the model, whereby the expected wage for unskilled laborers in the urban region is equal to the wage in the rural region. The probability of finding a job in the urban manufacturing sector is $\frac{a_{LM}X_M}{a_{LM}X_M + L_u}$ and the expected wage for unskilled laborers is therefore illustrated as $\frac{a_{LM}X_M}{a_{LM}X_M+L_u}w_u$. Therefore, the rural–urban migration equilibrium of unskilled labor presented is:

$$w_r = \frac{a_{LM}X_M}{a_{LM}X_M + L_u}w_u \tag{8}$$

Equivalently, the full employment condition of unskilled laborers could be written as:

$$a_{LF}X_F + a_{LP}X_P + \frac{W_u}{W_r}a_{LM}X_M = L \tag{9}$$

The endogenous variables in the system include w_r, w_u, r_F, r_p, r_M, X_F, X_p, and X_M. The parameters of the system are P_F, P_p, L, K_F, K_p, and K_M, which are exogenously given in the economy. The producers choose the minimum costs of producing a unit of product in the face of prevailing factor prices in the perfectly competitive factor market, and cost minimization entails that

$$w_r\,da_{LF} + r_F\,da_{KF} = 0 \tag{10}$$

$$w_r\,da_{LP} + r_P\,da_{KP} = 0 \tag{11}$$

$$w_u\,da_{LM} + r_M\,da_{KM} = 0 \tag{12}$$

The author borrows the same methodology from Jones (1971) to write these changes in relative terms:

$$\theta_{LF}\,\hat{a}_{LF} + \theta_{KF}\,\hat{a}_{KF} = 0 \tag{13}$$

$$\theta_{LP}\,\hat{a}_{LP} + \theta_{KP}\,\hat{a}_{KP} = 0 \tag{14}$$

$$\theta_{LM}\,\hat{a}_{LM} + \theta_{KM}\,\hat{a}_{KM} = 0 \tag{15}$$

where $\hat{a}_{LF} = \frac{da_{LF}}{a_{LF}}$, $\hat{a}_{LP} = \frac{da_{LP}}{a_{LP}}$ and $\hat{a}_{LM} = \frac{da_{LM}}{a_{LM}}$; $\theta_{LF} = \frac{w_r\,a_{LF}}{P_F}$, $\theta_{LP} = \frac{w_r\,a_{LP}}{P_P}$ and $\theta_{LM} = \frac{w_u\,a_{LM}}{1}$ represent factor distributive shares. To get the factor price changes, differentiation of Eqs. (1), (2), and (3) can be expressed as follows:

$$a_{LF}\,dw_r + a_{KF}\,dr_F = dP_F \tag{16}$$

$$a_{LP}\, dw_r + a_{KP}\, dr_P = dP_P \tag{17}$$

$$a_{LM}\, dw_u + a_{KM}\, dr_M = 0 \tag{18}$$

Substituting the relative terms into the above three differentiated equations yields

$$\theta_{LF}\,\widehat{w}_r + \theta_{KF}\,\widehat{r}_F = \widehat{P}_F \tag{19}$$

$$\theta_{LP}\,\widehat{w}_r + \theta_{KP}\,\widehat{r}_P = \widehat{P}_P \tag{20}$$

$$\theta_{LM}\,\widehat{w}_u + \theta_{KM}\,\widehat{r}_M = 0 \tag{21}$$

The above equations tell us that each commodity's relative price change is a weighted average of factor price changes, with the weights given by distributive shares reflecting the importance of each factor in unit costs. The results show that if the price of one product changes, the factor prices will alter unevenly.

The wage rate is determined by the full employment of unskilled laborers in the economy. The labor demand in each industry, written as $a_{LF}\,X_F$, $a_{LP}\,X_P$ and $a_{LM}\,X_M$, $X_i\,(i = F, P, M)$, depends on the output in each sector which is restricted by the availability of specific capital. Capital input requirement per unit output is denoted by a_{ki} for the three final tradable goods. Accordingly, the outputs of the three sectors can be written as $X_i = \frac{K_i}{a_{Ki}}$. The labor demands in the agricultural, processing, and manufacturing sectors are

$$L_F = a_{LF} X_F = \frac{a_{LF}}{a_{KF}} K_F \tag{22}$$

$$L_P = a_{LP} X_P = \frac{a_{LP}}{a_{KP}} K_P \tag{23}$$

$$L_M = a_{LM} X_M = \frac{a_{LM}}{a_{KM}} K_M \tag{24}$$

The total labor in the economy is

$$\frac{a_{LF}}{a_{KF}} K_F + \frac{a_{LP}}{a_{KP}} K_P + \frac{a_{LM}}{a_{KM}} K_M + L_u = L \tag{25}$$

Combining equations (22)–(24) and (9), we get the unskilled labor equilibrium condition of

$$\frac{a_{LF}}{a_{KF}} K_F + \frac{a_{LP}}{a_{KP}} K_P + \frac{W_u}{W_r} \frac{a_{LM}}{a_{KM}} K_M = L \tag{26}$$

The specific capital is fixed in each sector, but the wage rate for unskilled laborers may change. By separating the above unskilled labor equilibrium, where L is the total unskilled labor force in the economy, we get

$$\left(\frac{K_F da_{LF}}{L a_{KF}} - \frac{a_{LF} K_F da_{KF}}{L a_{KF}^2} \right) + \left(\frac{K_P da_{LP}}{L a_{KP}} - \frac{a_{LP} K_P da_P}{L a_{KP}^2} \right)$$
$$+ \left(\frac{dW_u}{W_r} - \frac{W_u dW_r}{w_r^2} \right) \frac{a_{LM}}{L a_{KM}} K_M$$
$$+ \frac{W_u}{W_r} \left(\frac{K_M da_{LM}}{L a_{KM}} - \frac{a_{LM} K_M da_{KM}}{L a_{KM}^2} \right) = \frac{dL}{L} \tag{27}$$

We define the fraction of the labor force in each sector as $\lambda_{Li} = \frac{a_{Li} X_i}{L}$ and the output in each industry as $X_i = \frac{K_i}{a_{Ki}}$. Then equation (27) can be written as follows:

$$\lambda_{LF}(\hat{a}_{LF} - \hat{a}_{KF}) + \lambda_{LP}(\hat{a}_{LP} - \hat{a}_{KP}) + \lambda_{LM} \left(\frac{dW_u}{W_r} - \frac{W_u dW_r}{w_r^2} \right)$$
$$+ \lambda_{LM} \frac{W_u}{W_r}(\hat{a}_{LM} - \hat{a}_{KM}) = \hat{L} \tag{28}$$

This can be rewritten as

$$\lambda_{LF}(\hat{a}_{LF} - \hat{a}_{KF}) + \lambda_{LP}(\hat{a}_{LP} - \hat{a}_{KP})$$
$$+ \lambda_{LM} \frac{W_u}{W_r}(\hat{w}_u - \hat{w}_r) + \lambda_{LM} \frac{W_u}{W_r}(\hat{a}_{LM} - \hat{a}_{KM}) = \hat{L} \tag{28.1}$$

In equilibrium, the wage rate must equal the value of unskilled labor's marginal product in each sector. The elasticities of labor's marginal product curves are defined as the relationship between real wage rate and the labor/capital ratio, expressed as

$$\gamma_{LF} = \frac{-(\hat{a}_{LF} - \hat{a}_{KF})}{\hat{w}_r - \hat{P}_F}, \gamma_{LP} = \frac{-(\hat{a}_{LP} - \hat{a}_{KP})}{\hat{w}_r - \hat{P}_P} \text{ and } \gamma_{LM} = -\frac{-(\hat{a}_{LM} - \hat{a}_{KM})}{w_u}$$

Substituting the elasticities into Eq. (28.1), we get

$$\lambda_{LF}\gamma_{LF}(\hat{w}_r - \hat{P}_F) + \lambda_{LP}\gamma_{LP}(\hat{w}_r - \hat{P}_P) + \lambda_{LM}\frac{W_u}{W_r}(\hat{w}_u - \hat{w}_r)$$

$$+ \lambda_{LM}\gamma_{LM}\frac{W_u}{W_r}\hat{w}_u = -\hat{L} \tag{29}$$

Rural–urban migration equilibrium of unskilled labor is presented as

$$w_r = \frac{a_{LM}X_M}{a_{LM}X_M + L_u}w_u,$$

Then, $\frac{W_u}{W_r} = \frac{1}{v}$ is the inverse of the employment ratio of unskilled labor in the urban region. Equation (29) can be rewritten as

$$\lambda_{LF}\gamma_{LF}(\hat{w}_r - \hat{P}_F) + \lambda_{LP}\gamma_{LP}(\hat{w}_r - \hat{P}_P)$$

$$+ \lambda_{LM}\frac{1}{v}(\hat{w}_u - \hat{w}_r) + \lambda_{LM}\gamma_{LM}\frac{1}{v}\hat{w}_u = -\hat{L} \tag{30}$$

Rearranging the above equation gives us the following:

$$\left(\lambda_{LF}\gamma_{LF} + \lambda_{LP}\gamma_{LP} - \lambda_{LM}\frac{1}{v}\right)\hat{w}_r + \left(\lambda_{LM}\frac{1}{v} + \lambda_{LM}\gamma_{LM}\frac{1}{v}\right)\hat{w}_u$$

$$= \lambda_{LF}\gamma_{LF}\hat{P}_F + \lambda_{LP}\gamma_{LP}\hat{P}_P - \hat{L} \tag{31}$$

Based on the employment condition ($w_r - vw_u = 0$), we can totally differentiate it to get

$$\hat{w}_r - \hat{w}_u = \hat{v} \tag{32}$$

The equations (19)–(21), (31), and (32) are expressed in the following matrix form:

$$
\begin{bmatrix}
\theta_{LF} & \theta_{KF} & 0 & 0 & 0 \\
\theta_{LP} & 0 & \theta_{KP} & 0 & 0 \\
0 & 0 & 0 & \theta_{LM} & \theta_{KM} \\
A & 0 & 0 & B & 0 \\
1 & 0 & 0 & 0 & -1
\end{bmatrix}
\begin{bmatrix}
\widehat{w}_r \\
\hat{r}_F \\
\hat{r}_p \\
\hat{r}_M \\
\widehat{w}_u
\end{bmatrix}
=
\begin{bmatrix}
\widehat{P}_F \\
\widehat{P}_P \\
0 \\
C \\
\hat{v}
\end{bmatrix}
\tag{33}
$$

where

$$
A = \left(\lambda_{LF}\gamma_{LF} + \lambda_{LP}\gamma_{LP} - \lambda_{LM}\frac{1}{v} \right) < 0
$$

$$
B = \left(\lambda_{LM}\frac{1}{v} + \lambda_{LM}\gamma_{LM}\frac{1}{v} \right) > 0
$$

$$
C = \lambda_{LF}\gamma_{LF}\widehat{P}_F + \lambda_{LP}\lambda_{LP}\widehat{P}_P - \widehat{L}
$$

Now let us investigate the effect of a change in the price of farm products on wage inequality. Firstly, we can solve equation (33) for $\widehat{w}_r$, $\widehat{w}_u$, $\hat{r}_F$, $\hat{r}_P$, and $\hat{r}_M$ with respect to $\widehat{P}_F$, by using the Cramer's rule[6]:

$$
\frac{\widehat{w}_r}{\widehat{P}_F} = \frac{\theta_{KP}\theta_{KF}\theta_{LM}\lambda_{LF}\gamma_{LF}}{\Delta} > 0
\tag{34}
$$

$$
\frac{\hat{r}_F}{\widehat{P}_F} = \frac{(-\theta_{KP}\theta_{KM}B - \theta_{KP}\theta_{LF}\theta_{LM}\lambda_{LF}\gamma_{LF} + A\theta_{LM})}{\Delta} > 0
\tag{35}
$$

$$
\frac{\hat{r}_P}{\widehat{P}_F} = \frac{-\theta_{KF}\theta_{LP}\theta_{LM}\lambda_{LF}\gamma_{LF}}{\Delta} < 0
\tag{36}
$$

---

[6] We follow Chaudhuri and Banerjee (2010) to solve the partial effects of changes in the farm product price on other variables.

$$\frac{\hat{r}_M}{\widehat{P}_F} = \frac{-\theta_{KM}\theta_{KF}\theta_{KP}\lambda_{LF}\gamma_{LF}}{\Delta} < 0 \qquad (37)$$

$$\frac{\widehat{w}_u}{\widehat{P}_F} = \frac{\theta_{KF}\theta_{KP}\theta_{LM}\lambda_{LF}\gamma_{LF}}{\Delta} > 0 \qquad (38)$$

where

$$\Delta = \theta_{KF}\theta_{KP}(-B\theta_{KM}) + \theta_{LM}A\theta_{KF}\theta_{KP} = -\left(\lambda_{LM}\frac{1}{v} + \lambda_{LM}\gamma_{LM}\frac{1}{v}\right)$$

$$\theta_{KF}\theta_{KP}\theta_{KM} + \theta_{KF}\theta_{KP}\theta_{LM}\left(\lambda_{LF}\gamma_{LF} + \lambda_{LP}\gamma_{LP} - \lambda_{LM}\frac{1}{v}\right) < 0$$

An agricultural import restriction policy that raises the domestic price shifts the value of the marginal product of labor in the agricultural sector upward to the line (*WU*) in Fig. 2.3. The farm sector expands due to the price increase, and the other two sectors reduce accordingly. Land owners gain, but capital owners in the other two sectors lose.[7] Simultaneously, the wage rate improves to w'_r due to the increase of the value of marginal product of labor in the farm sector. The wage rates of unskilled laborers in the other two sectors are enhanced as well due to the free mobility of that labor. Whether the unskilled wage rises enough to compensate for the higher cost of consuming the agricultural good will determine whether the real incomes of unskilled workers rise or fall.

Proposition 1: An increase in the price of the agricultural product may or may not raise the real incomes of unskilled laborers in rural and urban regions, depending on how important are farm products in their

---

[7] These predictions from the model are consistent with Jones' (1971) magnification effect. The return to land owners increases by more than the increase in the farm price. However, the reduction of returns to owners of capital in non-farm sectors is greater than the farm price change. It should be noted that we could compare the magnitude of changes in capital returns between the processing sector and the manufacturing sector if we do not add more assumptions here.

expenditure. The real return to land owners increases, while the real return to capital owners in both the processing sector and the manufacturing sector decrease.

In the above, only the agricultural subsidy scenario is examined. Prior to 2000, however, agriculture was taxed. In that case, domestic agricultural market prices were lowered for consumers but the wage rate was also lowered for unskilled laborers in the whole economy.

After 2000, agriculture, rural areas, and farmers[8] became more of a focus for the government. China's first document of 2015 has focused on agricultural reform for the 12th consecutive year (starting in 2004). The inequality of incomes between farm and non-farm households, the extent of rural poverty, unemployment in the rural area, and food security are serious concerns of the Chinese government, which sees improving domestic agricultural prices by applying trade restrictions as one way to appease farmers.

2.4 Political Support Model

By applying public policies, the government is trying to reallocate income between different agents to get the maximum political support from society, net of the political costs involved. A simple political support model that draws on the above income distribution model captures that notion. The key assumption is that rational political leaders maximize political credibility and support by supplying policies that interest groups desire.

2.4.1 *Model settings and predictions*

Different factor owners are assumed to belong to different interest groups. In China, earnings from farm land, in addition to earnings from their laboring, accrue to unskilled farm laborers. Skilled laborers, on the other hand, are assumed to receive the earnings not only

---

[8]These problems are called "three rural issues" by the Chinese government, a term that was first introduced into formal law in 2001.

of their skilled labor but also from specific physical capital used in the processing and manufacturing sectors.

We assume that all individuals have identical preferences and maximize an indirect utility function $U(y^i)$. y^i represents individual disposal net income, $i = F$, NF. Additionally, we assume that the farm and non-farm sectors each have n_i identical individuals with a pre-policy endowment income $\mathring{y}^i$. Finally, a politician has an agricultural price support policy R^i, representing the potential amount of income transfer from the non-farm sector to the farm sector, $R^L(R)$ represents the unskilled labor revenue from non-farm sectors for the agricultural sector individuals, and $R^C(R)$ represents the capital earnings of non-farm individuals. Thus, the net incomes of the farm individuals and non-farm individuals are as follows:

$$y^F = \mathring{y}^F + R^F = \{F(R) + R^L(R) - C[F(R) + R^L(R)]\}/n_F \qquad (39)$$

$$y^{NF} = \mathring{y}^{NF} + R^{NF} = -\{NF(R) + R^C(R) + C[NF(R) + R^C(R)]\}/n_{NF} \qquad (40)$$

where $C(-)$ represents the deadweight costs associated with transfer incomes, and we assume $C(0) = 0$, $C_R(R) > 0$ for $R > 0$, $C_R(R) < 0$, for $R > 0$, and $C_{RR}(R) > 0$. $C_R(R)$ and $C_{RR}(R)$ represent the first- and second-order derivatives of $C(-)$, respectively. The deadweight cost is an increasing function with respect to positive transfers and a decreasing function in terms of negative transfers. However, the deadweight cost functions show an increasing trend no matter whether the transfer value is positive or negative. n_F and n_{NF} are the number of individuals in the farm and non-farm sectors. The marginal effect of agricultural price support policy (R^i) on an individual's disposable income is calculated as follows by taking the first-order condition of their income with respect to the distorted agricultural policy:

$$\partial y^F/\partial R = [F_R(R) + R^L_R(R) - F_R(R)C_R(F(R)$$
$$+ R^L(R)) - R^L_R(R)C_R(F(R) + R^L(R))]/n_F \qquad (41)$$

$$\partial y^{NF}/\partial R = -[NF_R(R) + R_R^C(R) + NF_R(R)C_R(NF(R)$$
$$+ R^C(R)) + R_R^C(R)C_R(NF(R) + R^C(R))]/n_{NF} \quad (42)$$

Rearranging the first-order conditions yields the following:

$$\partial y^F/\partial R = [F_R(R) + R_R^L(R) - (F_R(R)$$
$$+ R_R^L(R))C_R(F(R) + R^L(R))]/n_F \quad (43)$$

$$\partial y^{NF}/\partial R = -[NF_R(R) + R_R^C(R) + (NF_R(R)$$
$$+ R_R^C(R))C_R(NF(R) + R^C(R))]/n_{NF} \quad (44)$$

We assume that individual's political support S^i is a strictly concave and increasing function of the change in utility caused by the agricultural trade-related policy, which is expressed as follows following the same structure as Swinnen (1994):

$$S^i = S(U^i(R) - U^i(0)) = S(V^i(R)) \quad (45)$$

The government maximizes the above total political support from the farm and non-farm sectors, subject to government budget constraints. The government objective function is to aggregate the political support from the individual level to the sectoral level in the farm and non-farm sectors:

$$\text{Max } n_F S(V^F(R)) + n_{NF}S(V^{NF}(R)) \quad (46)$$

Based on the effects of agricultural policy on the changes in individuals' income, we obtain the following equilibrium condition for the agricultural price support policy R^*:

$$\frac{S_V^F}{S_V^{NF}} =$$

$$-\frac{U_y^{NF}\left(NF_R(R) + R_R^C(R) + \left(NF_R(R) + R_R^C(R)\right)C_R\left(NF(R) + R^C(R)\right)\right)}{U_y^F\left(F_R(R) + R_R^L(R) - \left(F_R(R) + R_R^L(R)\right)C_R\left(F(R) + R^L(R)\right)\right)}$$

$$(47)$$

Rearranging the above condition yields

$$\frac{S_V^F}{S_V^{NF}} = -\frac{U_y^{NF}\left((1 + C_R(NF(R) + R^C(R)))\right)\left((NF_R(R) + R_R^C(R))\right)}{U_y^F\left((1 - C_R(F(R) + R^L(R)))\right)\left((F_R(R) + R_R^L(R))\right)} \quad (48)$$

The above equilibrium provides the optimal agricultural support policy between the two sectors by applying an optimal income transfer. The politically optimal condition means that the marginal increase in political support from those who benefit from the agricultural support policy equals the marginal decrease in political support from those who lose. This formula only considers the influence of the agricultural policy which leads to changes in factor incomes and a deadweight loss, not the original living situations and other influencing characteristics.

From the above equilibrium, we assume that the farm and non-farm sectors are identical ($\dot{y}^F = \dot{y}^{NF}$) before altering agricultural price support policies. That is, the optimal agricultural price support $R^* = 0$ and the political support equals unity: $S_V^F = S_V^{NF}$. Because political support functions are different between the two groups, the agricultural price support level will be different as well. From the above equilibrium, the endowment incomes of the agriculture sector and deadweight costs have effects on the determination of agricultural support policy as well. The optimal agricultural price support shifts toward individuals with more sensitive political support (Swinnen and Goter, 1993).

Proposition 2: *The political market equilibrium agricultural protection level is determined by balancing the marginal revenue of political supports from the farm sector and that from the non-farm sectors.*

2.4.2 *Illustration of political equilibrium*

The above model assumes the real reason for agriculture interventions is that they are 'created' (supplied) by the government or 'needed' (demanded) by some interest groups (mainly farmers), as illustrated in Fig. 2.4. The horizontal axis is the quantity of assistance to agriculture regarding RRA, which captures policy-induced distortions to *relative* agricultural prices. If the value of RRA is above zero,

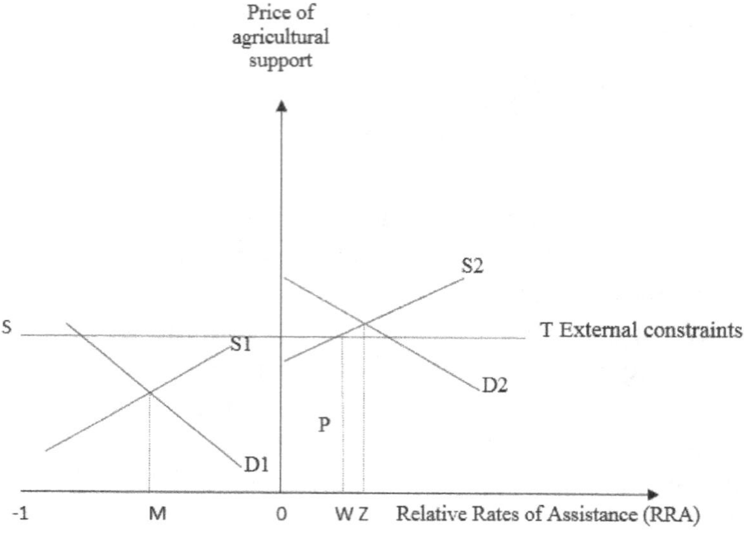

Fig. 2.4   Political market for agricultural protection.

it indicates that the agricultural sector is subsidized, or the government taxes the agricultural sector relative to the non-agricultural sectors. The vertical axis represents the "price" of a unit of assistance to agriculture. The demanders and the suppliers of the policy are potential beneficiaries. In the case of a distortionary price policy, the supply curve in this market represents the marginal political cost of providing an extra unit of protection to an industry, or of reduced political support from the groups opposed to such a policy change, while the demand curve represents the marginal return to political leaders in terms of political support from the groups seeking protection (Anderson and Hayami, 1986; Anderson, 1992; Shea, 2003). As for the equilibrium, given the government's objective function and the prevailing social interest structure, the equilibrium could be considered as an 'equilibrium price' solved in the political market with the participation of government and interest groups.

Before the late 1990s, the demand and supply of agricultural protection levels were lower. After 2000, both the demand and supply of agricultural support curves shifted, from S1–D1 to S2–D2.

After 2000, the domestic agricultural support was higher at Z, rather than W as previously.

2.4.3 *Determinants of partial political equilibrium*

The level of agricultural protection tends to increase in the course of economic development and structural changes in the economy. The equilibrium is determined simultaneously by government supply and interest groups' demand. With the development of the economy, the share of agriculture in GDP decreases, in China's case from 28% in 1978 to 10% in 2014. On average, each year the share has been decreasing over the past 36 years by 2–3 percentage points. The government does not have to boost the manufacturing sector at the expense of the agricultural sector at this stage. The price elasticity of food demand in the urban regions has become low, and the food expenditure share of the poor in urban regions has been declining over the past four decades. They are less politically sensitive to agricultural price increases now as compared with the 1980s.

According to the traditional political economy theory, a decrease in agricultural employment will lower the political cost of supplying higher agricultural protection. Once the absolute number of farmers also falls, so too do their collective action costs (Olson, 1965; Anderson, 1995a). For example, farm organizations can form to give farmers more power in arguing with the government to protect the agricultural sector. According to Ma and Abdulai (2016), cooperative membership could significantly improve farm household welfare.

The other three determinants of China's trade distortions are the poverty, inequality, and food security targets of the government. The inequality indicator, increasing from 29 in 1981 to 42 in 2010, reveals that the poverty gap within China has increased by 13 units. The poverty headcount ratio at \$1.90 a day (2011 PPP) accounted in 2010 for 11% of the population, and at \$3.10 a day for 27% (World Bank, 2016). As for food security, during food price upward spike periods, the Chinese government worries that food exporters may suddenly shutdown. The Chinese government has been keeping the food self-sufficiency level stable at around 98%, and never more than 10% away from 100% in the past two decades (Anderson and Strutt, 2014).

2.5 Conclusions

This chapter theoretically extends a two-sector specific-factors model in a dual economy into three sectors to better represent the economic structure of China. The model presents the simultaneous economic and political driving forces of China's changing agricultural protection levels. The results indicate that switching from taxing to subsidizing the agricultural sector depends on the changes of economic structure but even more critically on the underlying political support from heterogeneously interest groups in the course of economic development in a one-party polity. The Chinese government tries to seek the optimal political support from different interest groups by applying trade distortions, and even though distortionary agricultural policies would generate a dead weight loss in national economic welfare.

According to the theory of price distortion, taxing the agricultural sector has a large negative impact on agricultural production, and phasing out the trade distortions contributes to output increases and income improvement for farmers. However, the current high restrictions on imports are lowering resource allocation efficiency at the expense of national welfare and long-term economic growth (Anderson and Strutt, 2014). In addition, trade distortions cause higher consumer prices for food. According to the OECD report in 2013, China's consumer price of food is 15% higher than those at the border. Since Chinese households below the $1.25 international poverty line are on average net buyers of food (Anderson *et al.*, 2014), such agricultural price-support policies are probably adding to poverty in China.

More efficient policy instruments should be adopted that boost the agricultural sector without it being at the expense of national welfare, long-term economic growth, and poor consumer. Currently more than half of China's workers are in non-farm sectors and less than one-quarter currently work on farms (World Bank, 2012). Increasing rural education by initiating training programs for unskilled laborers could be an efficient way to improve their wage income.

From an institutional aspect, the government can further ease the unskilled labor market by Hukou System Reform and Rural Land Circulation Reform to address food security issues, persistent poverty, and inflated inequality between farm and non-farm households. Increasing agricultural productivity by technology innovation, decreasing trade transaction cost by infrastructure investment, and information communication improvement are other feasible approaches to solve the three rural issues, i.e., agriculture, rural regions, and farmers.

Determinants of Agricultural Protection Trends in China: Empirics

3.1 Introduction

Until the mid-1990s, anti-agricultural policies prevailed in China, and thereafter the government has been supporting the agricultural sector. According to the welfare effects of distortion theory[1] (Bhagwati, 1971; Harberger, 1971; Corden, 1971, 1997), removing price distortions — whether negative or positive — would improve social welfare.[2] However, China has rarely had neutral agricultural price and trade policies.

---

[1]Anderson *et al.* (2008) summarizes the concept of a market policy distortion as something that government imposes to create a gap between the marginal social return to sellers and the marginal social cost to buyers in a transaction.

[2]Removing agricultural policy distortions could improve national and global economic welfare, boost economic growth, and alleviate poverty and inequality (Milanovic, 2005; Anderson *et al.*, 2010), particularly for developing countries. Zhai and Hertel (2010) adopt a CGE model, taking China as a case study, to identify the effects of agricultural trade-related distortions on welfare, employment, and income

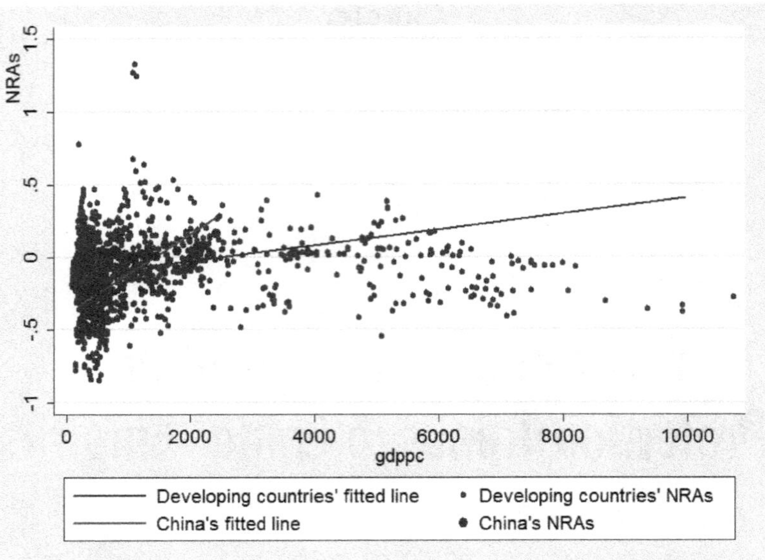

Fig. 3.1   NRAs and GDPPC, China and other developing countries.
Source: Anderson and Nelgen (2013).

The question of why agriculture is supported in rich countries and taxed in poor countries has received considerable attention in the literature (Anderson *et al.*, 2013). The question this chapter addresses is why the Chinese government has distorted its agricultural sector more than elsewhere, in both its anti-agricultural and pro-agricultural periods. Comparing the trend of China's agricultural protection level[3] with other developing countries as GDP per capita rises, it is clear in Fig. 3.1 that the Chinese government taxed the agricultural sector more heavily before the mid-1990s and assisted it more heavily thereafter relative to the average distortion level of other developing countries. This question is worth focusing on, partly as an extreme case study in the political economy of agricultural price distortions, and

---

distribution between different groups. In terms of large countries, they could improve social welfare by affecting the international market price and thus improving their terms of trade.

[3] We adopt the nominal rate of assistance (NRA) and the relative rate of assistance (RRA) as protection level indicators, defined in Anderson *et al.* (2008).

also because of the increasing importance of China in global agricultural markets.

To address this question, panel data compiled by Anderson and Nelgen (2013) on agricultural distortions are applied in this chapter. The results indicate that (1) arable land per capita, the proportion of the workforce in agriculture, and the agricultural self-sufficiency ratio explain more of the variance over time in China than in the rest of the world, and (2) income inequality plays a larger role than poverty in contributing to the variance of China's agricultural price distortions.

The rest of this chapter is organized as follows. Section 3.2 briefly reviews the related literature; Section 3.3 describes the data, methodology, and estimation methods; the results are summarized in Section 3.4; Section 3.5 provides robustness checks; and Section 3.6 concludes.

3.2 Literature Review

3.2.1 *Earlier literature*

The perspective of political economy provides a framework for analyzing the public policymaking process. The appealing theoretical models adopted to analyze agricultural trade-related policies can be briefly summarized as follows. Olson (1965) pioneered the role of collective actions to overcome the free-rider problem to influence the policy outcomes of the government. Numerous traditional political models, such as regulation theory (Stigler, 1971), group pressure theory (Becker, 1983, 1985), policy preference functions (Rausser and Freebairn, 1974), political support functions (Hillman, 1982), political preference functions (Bullock, 1994), and the conservative social welfare function (Corden, 1997), provide possible reasons why the government implements inefficient policies in different industries. Grossman and Helpman (1994) innovate the money contribution model, which provides effective micro-foundations for further trade protection policy analysis in democratic countries. This model becomes the workhorse theoretical tool to explain the trade policy formation process. In parallel with the political contribution model, the tariff formation function model (Findlay and Wellisz, 1982), the campaign contribution model (Magee *et al.*, 1989), the political support model (Rodrik, 1995), and the median voter model (Mayer, 1984) have been developed and adopted to analyze trade-related policies.

The government's agricultural trade policies can both increase social welfare and redistribute incomes between different interest groups (Rausser, 1982). The increase in agricultural protection in the course of economic development has been called a "developmental paradox" (Anderson and Hayami, 1986; Balisacan and Roumasset, 1987; Beghin and Kherallah, 1994; Swinnen *et al.*, 2000). A change in the structure of growing economies affects the costs and benefits of policy distortions to different interest groups (Anderson *et al.*, 2013). The agricultural protection level is higher with a smaller share of the workforce in farming (Swinnen, 1994; Garden, 1987; David and Huang, 1996; Honma and Hayami, 1987), a lower share of agriculture in GDP (Fulginiti and Shogren,1992), and lower productivity in agriculture (Honma and Hayami, 1987; de Gorter and Tsur, 1991). Agricultural protection will decrease with increases in food self-sufficiency (Swinnen, 1994), with falls in inequality between urban and rural households, and with decreases in poverty.

3.2.2 *Recent developments*

The theoretical contributions in the field of political economics concerning institutions and policymaking (Acemoglu and Robinson, 2006, 2012), limited access orders (North *et al.*, 2009), the role of constitutions (Persson and Tabellini, 2000), and electoral institutions (Besley and Persson, 2011) are furthering research in the political economy of agricultural policies. So too is the availability of the agricultural distortion data, particularly the set compiled by Anderson and Valenzuela (2008) and updated by Anderson and Nelgen (2013). Based on these new datasets, economists have sought to identify the effects of electoral rules, forms of government, institutions, and ideology of the government on agricultural trade-related policies (Anderson, 2010).

Regarding the ideology of the government, right-wing governments are more protectionist on average than left-wing governments (Olper, 2001; Dutt and Mitra, 2010). The results are consistent with the reality in France, where large farms and landowners are associated with right-wing political parties and small farms with left-wing parties (Swinnen, 2010a). However, the left wing tends to support farmers in unequal societies, and the relationship holds better in democracies than dictatorships (Olper, 2007). As for the institutions, democratization leads to a reduction of agricultural taxation and increases in agricultural subsidization or both, which is consistent with the predictions of the median voter model (Olper *et al.*, 2013).

As in democratic countries, communist autocracies too shift from taxing to subsidizing the agricultural sector in the course of their economic development (Rozelle and Swinnen, 2010). Agricultural policy reforms are determined by a complex interaction of majority voting rules and changes in the external environment (Pokrivcak *et al.*, 2006). Bates and Block (2010) point out that, in the absence of electoral party competition, agricultural taxation increases with the rural population share, and the existence of competition turns the lobbying disadvantage of the rural majority into a political advantage and reduces discrimination against the farm sector. Moreover, they find that taxation is more moderate if a country's leader comes from that region, and the government continues to tax export producers if it is a resource-rich country. Gawande and Hoekman (2010) find that a government facing strong electoral competition is more likely to subsidize their exports and engage in import protection, and the probability that exports will be taxed is greater, the greater the proportions of land that is arable and of the population that is rural.

From the world perspective, agricultural market policies intervene to different degrees across countries, products and year-to-year variations (Anderson *et al.*, 2013). Whether China, with its one-party government, differs from other countries has not been addressed before. In doing so in this chapter, we introduce government quality as an independent variable to explain the changes in agricultural policies.

3.3 Data and Methodology

3.3.1 *Variable descriptions and data sources*

In the main regressions, the dependent variable is the NRA, which is based largely on comparisons between domestic and international prices. The NRA is defined as the percentage by which government policies directly raise the gross return to producers of a product above what it would be without the government's intervention (or lower edit, if NRA < 0).

The NRA provided by the government for country i at time t is written NRA $= \frac{P_t - P_t^*}{P_t^*}$ as where P_t is the domestic price and P_t^* is the world market price at time t.

The other indicator, the Relative Rate of Assistance (RRA), is adopted as the outcome variable to do robustness checks. RRA captures policy-induced distortions to *relative* agricultural prices, and it is defined as

$$RRA = \left[\frac{1 + NRA_{ag^t}}{1 + NRA_{nonag^t}} - 1 \right]$$

where NRA_{ag^t} and NRA_{nonag^t} are, respectively, the percentage NRAs for the tradable parts of the agricultural and non-agricultural sectors. The World Bank provides estimates of annual policy-induced price distortions to agricultural incentives since 1955 (Anderson and Valenzuela, 2008; Anderson and Nelgen, 2013). This dataset accounts for between 92% and 95% of global GDP, population, and agricultural output and trade.

Table 3.1 presents all the variables and data sources. The independent variables are categorized into three groups, i.e., traditional economic factors, government preference indicators, and political contributors. Traditional economic variables mainly include GDP per capita, arable land per capita, employment share in the agricultural sector, and agricultural value added per worker. Agricultural value added per worker is from World Development Indicators (2012), and the other three variables are from the global distortions to agricultural incentives database (Anderson and Nelgen, 2013).

Table 3.1   List of variables and data sources.

Variable names	Data source
Dependent variables	
NRA	Anderson and Nelgen (2013)
RRA	Anderson and Nelgen (2013)
Independent variables	
Type 1: Standard controls	
GDP per capita	Anderson and Nelgen (2013)
Arable land per capita	Anderson and Nelgen (2013)
Employment share in agriculture	Anderson and Nelgen (2013)
Agricultural value added per worker	World Development Indicators (2012)
Type 2: Politically sensitive variables	
Self-sufficiency ratio	World Development Indicators (2012)
Lag of poverty 1	World Development Indicators (2012)
Lag of poverty 2	World Development Indicators (2012)
Lag of poverty 3	World Development Indicators (2012)
Lag of poverty 4	World Development Indicators (2012)
Lag of GINI coefficient	World Development Indicators (2012)
Lag of income inequality 1	World Development Indicators (2012)
Lag of income inequality 2	World Development Indicators (2012)
Type 3: Institutional quality measures	World Development Indicators (2012)
Democratic accountability	International Country Risk Guide (2013)
Government effectiveness	Institution quality Kaufmann World Bank (2013)
Political stability and absence of violence/terrorism	Institution quality Kaufmann World Bank (2013)
Regulatory quality	Institution quality Kaufmann World Bank (2013)
Control for corruption	Institution quality Kaufmann World Bank (2013)
Rule of law	Institution quality Kaufmann World Bank (2013)

Notes: Poverty ratio and income inequality are both measured by diversified indicators in the regression models and the data are from the same database.

Concerning the government's preference, a higher self-sufficiency ratio is the main target for the government to ensure food security, and poverty and inequality are the most politically sensitive determinants for the government in the agricultural trade policymaking process. Governments are reluctant to report self-sufficiency, poverty, and inequality conditions, so the data series are not continuous for most countries, leading to the sharp decrease of sample size in the regressions.

Four indicators are used to measure poverty: the poverty gap at $1.25 a day (PPP) (%)[4] (Poverty 1), the poverty gap at $2 a day (2005 PPP) (%) (Poverty 2), the poverty head count ratio at $1.25 a day (PPP) (% of population)[5] (Poverty 3), and the poverty head count ratio at $2 a day (PPP) (% of population) (Poverty 4). Having different types of indicators allows us to check the robustness of the estimated regression results.

Similarly, inequality is measured not only by GINI coefficients but also by two other indicators expressed as inequality 1 and inequality 2. Inequality 1 is calculated as the income share held by the highest 10% of the population divided by the income share held by the lowest 10% of the population, while inequality 2 refers to the highest and lowest 20% of the population.

The third group of independent variables includes democratic accountability,[6] government effectiveness, political stability and the absence of violence/terrorism, regulatory quality, control for corruption,

---

[4] Poverty gap at $1.25 a day (2005 PPP) (%) is the mean shortfall in income or consumption from the poverty line $1.25 a day (counting the non-poor as having zero shortfall), expressed as a percentage of the poverty line. This measure reflects the depth of poverty as well as its incidence.

[5] Poverty head count ratio at $1.25 a day is the percentage of the population living on less than $1.25 a day at 2005 international prices. As a result of revisions in PPP exchange rates, poverty rates for individual countries cannot be compared with poverty rates reported in earlier editions.

[6] Democratic accountability requires public bodies to be open and transparent in their dealings with the public and for government at all levels to explain and accept responsibility for its actions. Democratic accountability also entails government ensuring adequate opportunities.

and the rule of law. These are all politically related indicators that measure government institutions and institutional quality. To the best of the author's knowledge, this is the first time the effects of government institutional quality on policy outcomes have been tested in the field of political economy of agricultural trade-related policies. The democratic accountability indicator is from the International Country Risk Guide (2013) and the other five indicators measuring government institutional quality are from Kaufmann (2013). All the variables and data sources are listed in Table 3.1, and the summary statistics are in Table 3.2.

Table 3.2 Summary statistics.

Variable names	No. of obsv.	Mean	Std. dev.	Min	Max
NRAs	3169	0.2	0.6	−0.9	4.3
RRAs	2864	0.1	0.6	−0.9	4.1
Log (GDP per capita)	3071	7.7	1.7	4.5	10.7
Log (arable land per capita)	3199	−1.3	0.9	−3.4	1.3
Log (agricultural value added per worker)	1930	8.0	1.7	4.7	11.6
Self-sufficiency ratio	3169	1.3	0.8	0.0	15.8
Employment share in agriculture	3072	0.4	0.3	0.0	0.9
Lag of Poverty 1	430	6.8	10.2	0.0	53.1
Lag of Poverty 2	430	13.4	16.5	0.0	67.2
Lag of Poverty 3	431	18.0	23.4	0.0	86.1
Lag of Poverty 4	431	30.1	31.1	0.0	97.0
Lag of GINI coefficient	443	40.8	10.1	19.5	75.1
Lag of income inequality 1	448	21.0	27.4	3.3	36.1
Lag of income inequality 2	448	9.8	6.7	2.6	34.7
Democratic accountability	1851	4.3	1.6	0.0	6.0
Government effectiveness	937	0.4	1.0	−1.6	2.4
Regulatory quality	937	0.4	0.9	−2.2	2.1
Control for corruptions	936	0.3	1.1	−1.5	2.6
Rule of law	937	0.3	1.0	−1.8	2.0
Political stability and absence of violence/ terrorism	937	0.0	1.0	−2.7	1.7

Source: See Table 3.1.

3.3.2 *Estimation methodology*

The intent of this chapter is to measure the different driving forces affecting China's changing agricultural protection as compared with the ROW's. The interaction term (D_{it}), constructed by the product of China dummy variable (China$_t$) and one of the independent variables (X_{it}), is the main variable of interest in each regression, which is expressed in the following reduced form[7]:

$$Y_{it} = \pi_0 + \lambda D_{it} + \delta X_{it} + \mu_i + \mu_t + \sigma_{it} \tag{1}$$

- Y_{it} is the agricultural protection level measured by NRA, and RRA is applied in the robustness check regressions.
- D_{it} is the vector that is an interaction term constructed by the product of China dummy variable in period t (China$_t$) and one of the independent variables. The interaction terms are the main variables of interest.
- π_0 is a constant term.
- X_{it} refers to the vector of independent variables.
- μ_i is a generic representation of country fixed effects that capture all time-invariant country-specific characteristics and permanent differences.
- μ_t is a generic representation for time-varying macroeconomic shocks that affect the NRA identically.
- σ_{it} is the idiosyncratic error term.

To get the different elasticities for each determinant to compare China with the ROW, we analyze the effect of each interaction term (D_{it}), quantitatively, on the changes of agricultural protection levels. We control the main traditional determinants in the regressions as the benchmark.

---

[7] In each of the regression models, we apply the Hausman test to choose whether a fixed effects or random effects model should be used. In each test, we reject the null hypobook. This means the independent variables are correlated with the error term. Thus, two-way fixed effects should be used in all regressions in the later model estimation process.

3.3.3 *Estimation expectations*

The analysis begins with graphical views (Fig. 3.2) to see different driving forces of agricultural protection changes regarding GDP per capita (Panel A), the employment share of the agricultural sector (Panel B), the self-sufficiency ratio (Panel C), and income inequality (Panel D).

The lines from Panel A to Panel D represent the predicted NRA values by varying one of the determinants, and the black lines indicate the other countries' predicted NRA values. To test the difference between China and the ROW regarding GDP per capita, we see that the slope of China's fitted line is much steeper than the ROW's. China has much higher distortions than the world average in the process of economic development. With the decrease of employment share in the agricultural sector, the agricultural protection level in China increases more than the world average as shown in Panel B.

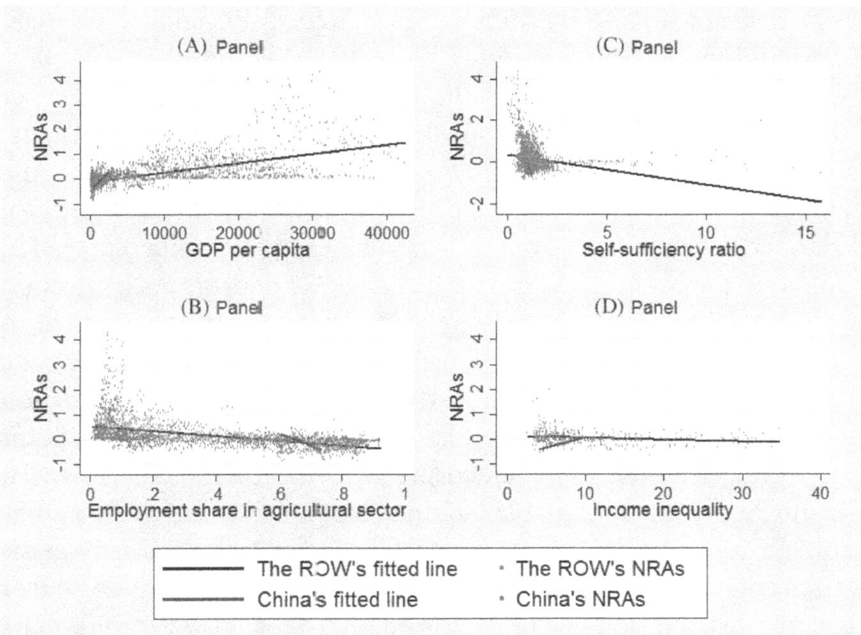

Fig. 3.2 Heterogeneous effects of determinants on agricultural protection between China and the rest of the world.

As the largest population and food consumption country, agricultural protection is most sensitive to food security conditions measured by a self-sufficiency ratio presented in Panel C. The slope of the income inequality indicator in China is much flatter in Panel D, and the slope is steeper than the world average.

3.4 Main Results

3.4.1 *Economic factors and the self-sufficiency ratio*

Columns 1–5 of Table 3.3 present the effects of traditional economic determinants and the self-sufficiency ratio on the changes of NRA. The benchmark control variables cover GDP per capita, arable land per capita, agricultural value added per worker, the self-sufficiency ratio, and the employment share in the agricultural sector. The variables of interest are the interaction terms between the China dummy variable and one of the determinants, as they indicate the determinants that are driving the differences in agricultural policy between China and the ROW.

With the improvement of the economy measured by GDP per capita, the agricultural protection level is increasing more for China. It indicates that the transformation from taxing to subsidizing the agricultural sector is sharper than the world average in the course of economic development. Concerning arable land per capita reported in column 2, the average effect on the changes of agricultural protection is not significant but negatively related. These results may be due to the improvement of agricultural technology during the past 30 years.

The arable land area is almost fixed, and agricultural distortion policies are not as sensitive to land compared with the significant effect of agricultural value added per worker (column 3). However, the interaction term of arable land per capita has a negatively significant effect (the partial F-test indicates that the effect for China is significantly different from the ROW) and the size is much higher than the average effect for the world. Arable land per capita plays a more important role in the formation of agricultural policy in China than in the ROW, perhaps because other countries (particularly

Table 3.3 Nominal rates of assistance and economic determinants.

Variables	(1) NRAs	(2) NRAs	(3) NRAs	(4) NRAs	(5) NRAs
China × Log (GDP per capita)	0.172**	—	—	—	—
	(0.082)	—	—	—	—
China × Log (arable land per capita)		-1.055**	—	—	—
		(0.488)	—	—	—
China × Log (agri-value added per worker)			0.424**	—	—
			(0.203)	—	—
China × Employment share in agriculture				-2.918**	—
				(1.439)	—
China × Self-sufficiency ratio					-1.316**
					(0.622)
Log (GDP per capita)	0.278***	0.296***	0.280***	0.283***	0.293***
	(0.100)	(0.093)	(0.099)	(0.098)	(0.094)
Log (arable land per capita)	-0.107	-0.101	-0.107	-0.106	-0.106
	(0.096)	(0.095)	(0.096)	(0.096)	(0.096)
Log (agricultural value added per worker)	-0.272**	-0.275**	-0.272**	-0.273**	-0.274**
	(0.108)	(0.109)	(0.108)	(0.108)	(0.108)
Self-sufficiency ratio	-0.045***	-0.046***	-0.045***	-0.045***	-0.046***
	(0.015)	(0.015)	(0.015)	(0.015)	(0.015)
Employment share in agriculture	-2.920***	-2.914***	-2.919***	-2.917***	-2.923***
	(0.929)	(0.931)	(0.929)	(0.930)	(0.931)
Number of observations	1860	1860	1860	1860	1860
Number of countries	74	74	74	74	74
Country fixed effects	Yes	Yes	Yes	Yes	Yes
Year fixed effects	Yes	Yes	Yes	Yes	Yes
Adj. R^2	0.237	0.237	0.237	0.237	0.237

Notes: (1) Robust standard errors are reported in the parentheses; (2) *significant at 10%; **significant at 5%; ***significant at 1%; (3) Year dummies are not reported.

developed countries) have higher levels of agricultural technology than China. Column 3 shows that agricultural value added per worker has opposite effects on agricultural distortion formation. This may be because the rapid switch from taxing to subsidizing the agricultural sector induced rapid agricultural productivity growth.

The employment share in the agricultural sector has the highest weight compared with other determinants reported in column 4. The effect of China's employment share in the agricultural sector is almost twice the world average. This may be because China's government is keen to keep farmers in the agricultural sector but is very sensitive to social instability in rural areas.

On average, a 1 percentage point decrease in the self-sufficiency ratio causes the NRA to increase by 0.046 points, as reported in column 5. In China, the absolute size of this effect is almost 30 times higher than the world average. The government knows from historical experience that social stability depends on there being enough food. Alao, traditional Chinese culture plays a role, as captured in the old proverb "to the Country people are all-important, to the people food stuff is all-important, and to the food stuff safety is all-important".

3.4.2 *Poverty and inequality*

Poverty and inequality are the most politically sensitive determinants in China's agricultural trade policymaking process. Unfortunately, the sample size drops sharply in these regressions as mentioned in Section 3.3.1. In order to solve this endogeneity issue, this chapter applied the lagged value of poverty in the regressions to reduce the reverse causality problem. In addition, the lagged variables are potentially correlated with the error term. The two-way fixed panel model could deal with the omitted variables, including country fix effect and common macroeconomic shocks. As robustness checks, four indicators are used to measure poverty, each lagged one year to alleviate endogeneity. In this part, due to the high collinearity between GDP and poverty in developing countries,[8] the economic growth indicator is dropped in the regressions in Table 3.4.

From columns 1–4, the poverty indicators are poverty gap at $1.25 a day (PPP) (%), poverty gap at $2 a day (PPP) (%), poverty

---

[8] The high pairwise correlation coefficient between GDP per capita in logarithm value and the lag of Poverty 1 has reached –0.7339, and it is statistically significant at 1%.

Table 3.4 Nominal rates of assistance and poverty ratio.

Variables	(1) NRAs	(2) NRAs	(3) NRAs	(4) NRAs
Lag of Poverty 1	0.002	—	—	—
	(0.004)	—	—	—
China × Lag of Poverty 1	−0.013***	—	—	—
	(0.003)	—	—	—
Lag of Poverty 2		0.001	—	—
		(0.003)	—	—
China × Lag of Poverty 2		−0.009***	—	—
		(0.003)	—	—
Lag of Poverty 3			0.001	—
			(0.002)	—
China × Lag of Poverty 3			−0.006***	—
			(0.002)	—
Lag of Poverty 4				−0.000
				(0.002)
China × Lag of Poverty 4				−0.006***
				(0.002)
Log (arable land per capita)	0.047	0.044	0.044	0.039
	(0.139)	(0.138)	(0.138)	(0.135)
Log (agricultural value added per worker)	0.051	0.054	0.054	0.060
	(0.092)	(0.095)	(0.096)	(0.093)
Self-sufficiency ratio	−0.048***	−0.048***	−0.048***	−0.048***
	(0.004)	(0.004)	(0.004)	(0.004)
Employment share in agriculture	−0.456	−0.505	−0.512	−0.481
	(0.932)	(0.895)	(0.883)	(0.863)
Number of observations	389	389	390	390
Number of countries	48	48	49	49
Country fixed effects	Yes	Yes	Yes	Yes
Year fixed effects	Yes	Yes	Yes	Yes
Adj. R^2	0.152	0.153	0.153	0.154

Notes: (1) Robust standard errors are reported in the parentheses; (2) *significant at 10%; **significant at 5%; ***significant at 1%; (3) Year dummies are not reported.

head count ratio at \$1.25 a day (PPP) (% of population), and poverty head count ratio at \$2 a day (PPP) (% of population). The coefficients on the interaction of China with the lag of poverty indicators are all negative[9] and significant at 1%. However, the average poverty effect on NRA in the world is not significant, and its size is close to zero. Poverty plays a larger role in determining changes of agricultural protection policies in China than in the ROW. However, the partial F-test (including lagged poverty and the interaction of China with lagged poverty) is not significant, based on the benchmark controls and two-way fixed effects with robust standard errors. The role of poverty in determining government's agricultural distortions is found to be not significant.

Previous political economy research studies found that countries which experience a higher level of inequality exhibit a higher level of agricultural protection (Dutt and Mitra, 2010). Table 3.5 reports the effects of inequality on the government's agricultural policies in China compared with the ROW. Column 1 introduces the GINI coefficient into the regression, and it shows that on average inequality has no effect on the changes in agricultural protection. The coefficient on the interaction of the China dummy with the lagged GINI coefficient is positive[10] and significant at 1%. The joint effect of the GINI coefficient and the interaction term on the changes of agricultural protection passes the partial F-test. Column 2 uses the lagged value of inequality 1 as the inequality indicator, and the result is still robust. When introducing inequality 2 into the regression model reported in column 3, the effect size is twice the first two regression results, and it passes the partial F-test as well. The other econometric problem is measurement error for inequality, which will attenuate the slope of the coefficient in the least squares regression toward zero. However, this regression result gives robust evidence that suggests inequality indeed has the effect on agricultural policy formation in China.

---

[9] The correlation between poverty and NRA is negative at time-period t with no lag variable.

[10] The correlation between NRA and the interaction term between China and Gini coefficient is positive at time period t.

Table 3.5 Nominal rates of assistance and income inequality.

Variables	(1) NRAs	(2) NRAs	(3) NRAs
Lag of GINI coefficient	−0.001	—	—
	(0.004)	—	—
China × Lag of GINI coefficient	0.033***	—	—
	(0.006)	—	—
Lag of income inequality 1		0.000	—
		(0.000)	—
China × Lag of income inequality 1		0.033***	—
		(0.005)	—
Lag of income inequality 2		—	−0.001
		—	(0.005)
China × Lag of income inequality 2		—	0.074***
		—	(0.012)
Log (arable land per capita)	0.042	0.032	0.033
	(0.130)	(0.131)	(0.131)
Log (agricultural value added per worker)	0.032	0.041	0.035
	(0.090)	(0.091)	(0.089)
Self-sufficiency ratio	−0.050***	−0.049***	−0.049***
	(0.004)	(0.004)	(0.004)
Employment share in agriculture	−0.716	−0.606	−0.640
	(0.762)	(0.808)	(0.787)
Number of observations	397	402	402
Number of countries	64	66	66
Country fixed effects	Yes	Yes	Yes
Year fixed effects	Yes	Yes	Yes
Adj. R^2	0.172	0.156	0.158

Notes: (1) Robust standard errors are reported in the parentheses; (2) *significant at 10%; **significant at 5%; ***significant at 1%; (3) Year dummies are not reported.

China is a one-party-ruled government and has a strong preference to stabilize society, ensure alleviation of poverty, and reduce inequality. The evidence in this part shows that the Chinese government cares more about inequality than poverty in the agricultural policymaking process. Inequality is more likely to induce regional unrest and social instability and threaten the power of the Chinese government. As the old proverb states "inequality, not scarcity persecutes governors; anarchy, not poverty haunts them". This is consistent with the previous study which asserts that inequality aversion is the reason less skilled, intensive industries tend to receive relatively high levels of trade protection in China (Lü *et al.*, 2012).

3.4.3 *Political contributors*

Political institutions have attracted tremendous attention in determining government agricultural trade-related policies either in developing countries or developed countries. China is a one-party country, and the institutional quality (Polity 2) variable has had a value of negative 7 each year from 1977 to 2012, which will not be used in this book. Thus, we apply five other indicators as discussed in Part 3.3.1 which are potentially the best institutional indicators to apply in our empirical analysis.

Table 3.6 presents the negative effects of three institutional indicators on the changes of agricultural protection policies. Column 1 reports the effect of democratic accountability and the effect size is 0.062, which is statistically significant at 1%. On average, with an increase in democracy, the agricultural protection level keeps the same direction. As for China, agricultural protection is declining with increases in democracy. Columns 2 and 3 show the effects of institutional quality on distorted agricultural policies. On average, the effect is not significant for government effectiveness, nor for the rule of law. For China, the effect of government effectiveness is weak and the rule of law has no significant effect, both of which are negative.

Table 3.7 further reports the effects of institutional quality on agricultural policies using three other indicators, including regulatory quality (column 1), controls for corruption (column 2), and political stability and absence of violence (column 3).

From the perspective of the world as a whole, institution quality has a positive effect, and the result is consistent with the results shown

Table 3.6 Nominal rates of assistance and political institution quality.

Variables	(1) NRAs	(2) NRAs	(3) NRAs
Democratic accountability	0.062***	—	—
	(0.017)	—	—
China × Democratic accountability	−0.174***	—	—
	(0.058)	—	—
Government effectiveness	—	0.011	—
	—	(0.051)	—
China × Government effectiveness	—	−0.287*	—
	—	(0.165)	—
Rule of law	—	—	0.081
	—	—	(0.057)
China × Rule of law	—	—	−0.185
	—	—	(0.138)
Log (GDP per capita)	0.307***	0.423***	0.371***
	(0.115)	(0.108)	(0.083)
Log (arable land per capita)	−0.055	−0.051	−0.051
	(0.095)	(0.096)	(0.094)
Log (agricultural value added per worker)	−0.273**	−0.091	−0.087
	(0.133)	(0.085)	(0.083)
Self-sufficiency ratio	−0.043***	−0.038***	−0.038***
	(0.013)	(0.004)	(0.004)
Employment share in agriculture	−3.582***	−3.166***	−3.387***
	(1.205)	(1.057)	(1.144)
Number of observations	1607	802	802
Number of countries	72	74	74
Country fixed effects	Yes	Yes	Yes
Year fixed effects	Yes	Yes	Yes
Adj. R^2	0.266	0.320	0.323

Notes: (1) Robust standard errors are reported in the parentheses; (2) *significant at 10%; **significant at 5%; ***significant at 1%; (3) Year dummies are not reported.

Table 3.7   Nominal rates of assistance and political institution quality.

Variables	(1) NRAs	(2) NRAs	(3) NRAs
Regulatory quality	0.089*	—	—
	(0.049)	—	—
China × Regulatory quality	0.149*	—	—
	(0.085)	—	—
Control for corruptions		0.040	—
		(0.045)	—
China × Control for corruptions		0.294**	—
		(0.129)	—
Political stability and absence of violence			0.044*
			(0.025)
China × Political stability and absence of violence			0.160
			(0.130)
Log (GDP per capita)	0.376***	0.413***	0.381***
	(0.084)	(0.090)	(0.087)
Log (arable land per capita)	−0.034	−0.050	−0.044
	(0.095)	(0.098)	(0.095)
Log (agricultural value added per worker)	−0.105	−0.094	−0.083
	(0.080)	(0.085)	(0.085)
Self-sufficiency ratio	−0.037***	−0.037***	−0.038***
	(0.004)	(0.004)	(0.004)
Employment share in agriculture	−3.336***	−3.174***	−3.352***
	(1.091)	(1.073)	(1.064)
Number of observations	802	802	802
Number of countries	74	74	74
Country fixed effects	Yes	Yes	Yes
Year fixed effects	Yes	Yes	Yes
Adj. R^2	0.326	0.322	0.324

Notes: (1) Robust standard errors are reported in the parentheses; (2) *significant at 10%; **significant at 5%; ***significant at 1%; (3) Year dummies are not reported.

in Table 3.6. The coefficients on the interactions of the China dummy with the three institutional quality indicators are all positive, and political stability and the absence of violence have no significant effect. For the political contributors, on average, the coefficient between institution quality and agricultural policies is positive. Regarding China, due to the different functions of the institutional indicators, their effects reveal positive or negative signs, respectively.

3.5 Robustness Checks

Some robustness checks have been done in the empirical analysis in the above part, using lag variables and applying different indicators for inequality, poverty, and institution quality. It is possible that the government could assist farming even when it does not change the NRA for agricultural products, namely, by lowering assistance to non-agricultural sectors. Thus, we test the Relative Rate of Assistance (RRA) as the endogenous variable in this section.

Applying the same methodology with two-way fixed effects, Table A.1 in the Appendix reports the effects of the traditional economic determinants and the self-sufficiency ratio on RRA. From column 1 to column 5, the interactions of the China dummy with GDP per capita, arable land per capita, agricultural value added per worker, the share of employment in the agricultural sector, and the self-sufficiency ratio are introduced into the regression one by one. All the effect sizes of the five influencing factors increase, and the signs are consistent with the estimated results shown in Table 3.3 when controlling all the benchmark variables. For the traditional variable, the self-sufficiency ratio becomes insignificant from the perspective of the world.

Tables A.2 and A.3 in the Appendix report the effects of poverty and inequality on RRA, respectively. From column 1 to column 4 in Table A.2, the poverty indicators are the poverty gap at $1.25 a day (PPP) (%), poverty gap at $2 a day (PPP) (%), poverty head count ratio at $1.25 a day (PPP) (% of population), and poverty head count ratio at $2 a day (PPP) (% of population). They are introduced into the regression one by one. All the coefficients of the interaction of the China dummy with the lagged poverty indicators continue to be negative and significant at 1%, and all of the effect sizes increase compared with the results in Table 3.4.

Table A.3 shows the effects of inequality on RRA by applying the same inequality indicators, including the GINI coefficient, inequality 1, and inequality 2. The coefficients on the interactions of the China dummy with inequality indicators show that agricultural protection becomes higher with the growth of the inequality compared with the results in Table 3.5. Again, inequality has more influence on China's agricultural protection than poverty.

Tables A.4 and A.5 in the Appendix report the effects on RRA of the interaction of the China dummy with political influencing factors. The coefficients of interaction terms become insignificant, except democratic accountability. This may be because democratic accountability is a proxy for institutions, and all the other variables are indicators of institutional quality. Thus, there is no robust evidence to indicate that institutional quality has a significant effect on agricultural policy when considering non-agricultural policies.

3.6 Conclusions

China's changing agricultural protection levels are explained by a multiplicity of factors: (1) China's changing agricultural protection levels are closely linked to economic development and structural changes; (2) inequality and poverty have opposite effects on China's changing agricultural protection policy formation; and (3) institutional quality has not been influencing China's agricultural price and trade policies.

Arable land per capita, the proportion of the workforce in the agricultural sector, and the self-sufficiency ratio explain more of China's policy than that of the ROW. Inequality has a stronger influence than poverty in contributing to the variance in China's agricultural protection. Although we could not strictly claim that our findings are causal effects, the results are confirmed when using the relative rate of assistance as the alternative agricultural protection indicator.

Appendix

Table A.1   Relative rates of assistance and economic determinants.

Variables	(1) RRAs	(2) RRAs	(3) RRAs	(4) RRAs	(5) RRAs
China × Log (GDP per capita)	0.211**	—	—	—	—
	(0.084)	—	—	—	—
China × Log (arable land per capita)	−1.303**	—	—	—	
	(0.494)	—	—	—	
China × Log (agri-value added per worker)		0.525**	—	—	
		(0.207)	—	—	
China × Employment share in agriculture			−3.705**	—	
			(1.458)	—	
China × Self-sufficiency ratio				−1.565**	
				(0.644)	
Log (GDP per capita)	0.258**	0.281***	0.260**	0.262**	0.280***
	(0.106)	(0.099)	(0.105)	(0.104)	(0.101)
Log (arable land per capita)	−0.096	−0.087	−0.095	−0.094	−0.094
	(0.118)	(0.117)	(0.118)	(0.118)	(0.118)
Log (agricultural value added per worker)	−0.328***	−0.332***	−0.328***	−0.329***	−0.331***
	(0.117)	(0.117)	(0.117)	(0.117)	(0.117)
Self-sufficiency ratio	−0.012	−0.013	−0.012	−0.012	−0.013
	(0.011)	(0.011)	(0.011)	(0.011)	(0.011)
Employment share in agriculture	−2.705***	−2.695***	−2.703***	−2.700***	−2.705***
	(0.919)	(0.922)	(0.919)	(0.920)	(0.921)
Number of observations	1687	1687	1687	1687	1687
Number of countries	68	68	68	68	68
Country fixed effects	Yes	Yes	Yes	Yes	Yes
Year fixed effects	Yes	Yes	Yes	Yes	Yes
Adj. R^2	0.232	0.231	0.232	0.232	0.231

Notes: (1) Robust standard errors are reported in the parentheses; (2) *significant at 10%; **significant at 5%; ***significant at 1%; (3) Year dummies are not reported.

Table A.2   Relative rates of assistance and poverty ratio.

Variables	(1) RRAs	(2) RRAs	(3) RRAs	(4) RRAs
Lag of Poverty 1	−0.001	—	—	—
	(0.004)	—	—	—
China × Lag of Poverty 1	−0.015***	—	—	—
	(0.003)	—	—	—
Lag of Poverty 2		−0.001	—	—
		(0.003)	—	—
China × Lag of Poverty 2		−0.011***	—	—
		(0.003)	—	—
Lag of Poverty 3			−0.001	—
			(0.002)	—
China × Lag of Poverty 3			−0.007***	—
			(0.002)	—
Lag of Poverty 4				−0.001
				(0.002)
China × Lag of Poverty 4				−0.007***
				(0.002)
Log (arable land per capita)	0.083	0.085	0.085	0.088
	(0.116)	(0.116)	(0.117)	(0.115)
Log (agricultural value added per worker)	−0.080	−0.083	−0.083	−0.088
	(0.093)	(0.095)	(0.097)	(0.095)
Self-sufficiency ratio	−0.015***	−0.016***	−0.016***	−0.016***
	(0.004)	(0.004)	(0.004)	(0.004)
Employment share in agriculture	−0.757	−0.767	−0.767	−0.719
	(0.755)	(0.728)	(0.724)	(0.714)
Number of observations	363	363	363	363
Number of countries	45	45	45	45
Country fixed effects	Yes	Yes	Yes	Yes
Year fixed effects	Yes	Yes	Yes	Yes
Adj. R^2	0.218	0.224	0.225	0.227

Notes: (1) Robust standard errors are reported in the parentheses; (2) *significant at 10%; **significant at 5%; ***significant at 1%; (3) Year dummies are not reported.

Table A.3 Relative rates of assistance and income inequality.

Variables	(1) RRAs	(2) RRAs	(3) RRAs
Lag of GINI coefficient	−0.003	—	—
	(0.005)	—	—
China × Lag of GINI coefficient	0.041***	—	—
	(0.007)	—	—
Lag of income inequality 1	—	0.000	—
	—	(0.000)	—
China × Lag of inequality 1	—	0.042***	—
	—	(0.005)	—
Lag of income inequality 2	—	—	−0.002
	—	—	(0.004)
China × Lag of income inequality 2	—	—	0.093***
	—	—	(0.013)
Log (arable land per worker)	0.102	0.090	0.093
	(0.110)	(0.112)	(0.111)
Log (agricultural value added per worker)	−0.125	−0.110	−0.121
	(0.098)	(0.103)	(0.105)
Self-sufficiency ratio	−0.018***	−0.016***	−0.017***
	(0.005)	(0.004)	(0.004)
Employment share in agriculture	−0.824	−0.735	−0.775
	(0.633)	(0.692)	(0.668)
Number of observations	369	373	373
Number of countries	60	61	61
Country fixed effects	Yes	Yes	Yes
Year fixed effects	Yes	Yes	Yes
Adj. R^2	0.243	0.223	0.227

Notes: (1) Robust standard errors are reported in the parentheses; (2) *significant at 10%; **significant at 5%; ***significant at 1%; (3) Year dummies are not reported.

Table A.4   Relative rates of assistance and political quality.

Variables	(1) RRAs	(2) RRAs
Regulatory quality	0.062	—
	(0.049)	—
China × Regulatory quality	0.142	—
	(0.086)	—
Control for corruption		0.020
		(0.045)
China × Control for corruption		0.139
		(0.113)
Log (GDP per capita)	0.298***	0.323***
	(0.076)	(0.083)
Log (arable land per capita)	0.041	0.031
	(0.109)	(0.109)
Log (agricultural-value added per worker)	−0.203**	−0.194**
	(0.087)	(0.091)
Self-sufficiency ratio	−0.009	−0.009
	(0.006)	(0.006)
Employment share in agriculture	−3.537***	−3.440***
	(1.072)	(1.067)
Number of observations	733	733
Number of countries	68	68
Country fixed effects	Yes	Yes
Year fixed effects	Yes	Yes
Adj. R^2	0.315	0.312

Notes: (1) Robust standard errors are reported in the parentheses; (2) *significant at 10%; **significant at 5%; ***significant at 1%; (3) Year dummies are not reported.

Table A.5 Relative rates of assistance and institutional quality.

Variables	(1) RRAs	(2) RRAs	(3) RRAs	(4) RRAs
Democratic accountability	0.043**	—	—	—
	(0.016)	—	—	—
China × Democratic accountability	-0.177***	—	—	—
	(0.051)	—	—	—
Government effectiveness		0.012	—	—
		(0.054)	—	—
China × Government effectiveness		-0.108	—	—
		(0.152)	—	—
Rule of law			0.011	—
			(0.048)	—
China × Rule of law			-0.153	—
			(0.124)	—
Political stability and absence of violence				0.027
				(0.022)
China × Political stability and absence of violence				-0.033
				(0.118)
Log (GDP per capita)	0.267**	0.323***	0.321***	0.298***
	(0.114)	(0.096)	(0.075)	(0.084)
Log (arable land per capita)	-0.054	0.030	0.031	0.034
	(0.129)	(0.107)	(0.108)	(0.106)
Log (agricultural value added per worker)	-0.312**	-0.193**	-0.192**	-0.190**
	(0.140)	(0.090)	(0.089)	(0.089)
Self-sufficiency ratio	-0.012	-0.010	-0.009	-0.010
	(0.011)	(0.006)	(0.006)	(0.006)
Employment share in agriculture	-3.472***	-3.432***	-3.450***	-3.541***
	(1.173)	(1.049)	(1.103)	(1.077)
Number of observations	1489	733	733	733
Number of countries	68	68	68	68
Country fixed effects	Yes	Yes	Yes	Yes
Year fixed effects	Yes	Yes	Yes	Yes
Adj. R^2	0.245	0.312	0.311	0.313

Notes: (1) Robust standard errors are reported in the parentheses; (2) *significant at 10%; **significant at 5%; ***significant at 1%; (3) Year dummies are not reported.

Geographic Politics, Loss Aversion, and Trade Policy: The Case of Cotton and China

4.1 Introduction

China's cotton policy attracts attention internationally due to its cotton industry's substantial role in the world cotton market, and domestically because of where it is produced in China. Since 2005, the share of China's cotton production in Xinjiang has been continuously increasing and now exceeds 50%. China's cotton trade protection, measured by Nominal Rates of Assistance (NRA),[1] fluctuates at a higher degree between 2005 and 2015 (Fig. 4.1). This chapter seeks to explain that change, drawing on the approach used by Freund and Özden (2008), who extend the Grossman and Helpman model (1994) (G–H model hereafter) incorporating agents' preferences

---

[1] It is expressed as NRA $= \frac{P_t - P_t^*}{P_t^*}$ where P_t is the domestic price and P_t^* is the border price at time t.

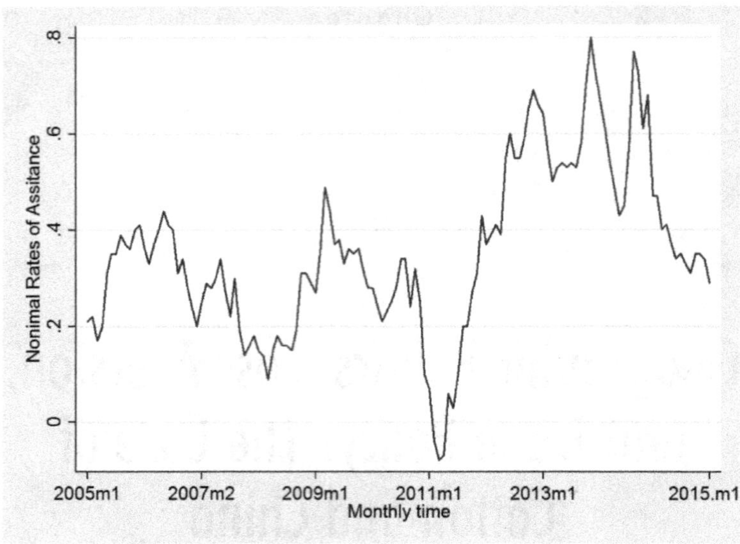

Fig. 4.1   Cotton trade protection in China, January 2005–January 2015.

characterizing loss aversion and reference dependence in a small open economy. More specifically, we seek to understand the Chinese government's trade policy responses to international price fluctuations by taking cotton as a case study.

In addition to shedding light on the specific case of cotton in China, this chapter contributes to the literature in two other ways. First, it specifies the government's objective function as the sum of political support and the aggregate social welfare for a non-democracy characterized with sensitive geographic dimensions to interest group politics. It thus goes beyond the monetary contribution model of Grossman and Helpman (1994). And second, it considers two cases (when the world price is higher, as well as when it is lower, than a reference price), therefore going beyond Freund and Özden (2008) who only consider a world price slump.

The structure of this chapter is as follows. Section 4.2 summaries the pertinent literature. Factual background information on China's cotton production, Xinjiang's geographic position, and cotton trade policies is summarized in Section 4.3. Section 4.4 develops the theoretical model and extends it from a small country to a large country.

China's cotton trade policy is used to empirically test the model in Section 4.5, and Section 4.6 concludes.

4.2 Literature Review

4.2.1 *Political incentives driving inefficient and suboptimal policies*

The perspective of political economy provides a framework for politicians and economists to uncover the formation of and variations over time in policy interventions. Various branches of thought, dating back to the 1960s, have given insight into the interactions of economic and political forces among different interest groups affecting the policy equilibrium. Among the important contributions, Olson (1965) pioneered the role of collective actions to overcome the free-rider problem to influence policy outcomes of government. Numerous other traditional political models, including regulation theory (Stigler, 1971), pressure group theory (Becker, 1983, 1985), policy preference functions (Rausser and Freebairn, 1974), political support functions (Hillman, 1982), political preference functions (Bullock, 1994), and the conservative social welfare function (Corden, 1997), seek to explain the reasons why governments implement inefficient distorted policies in different sectors. In the case of agricultural policies, the arable land endowment per worker, the employment share in the agricultural sector, terms of trade for agriculture, the share of agriculture in GNP, and the share of food in total expenditure are discussed based on collective action by different interest groups (Anderson and Hayami, 1986; Rausser, 1982). Other factors including low farm incomes, slow farm productivity growth, and low supply and demand elasticities are also emphasized (Gardner, 1987).

Grossman and Helpman (1994) improved the interest group model by providing microeconomic foundations, such that it became the workhorse tool to explain trade policy formation. Based on the G–H model, a preference for inequality aversion is introduced into an individual's utility function (Lü *et al.*, 2012). This comparative static model was followed by a dynamic political economy model with overlapping generations, heterogeneous agents, endogenous human capital investment, and costly worker adjustment (Blanchard and Willmann, 2013), and used to analyze the protectionist overshooting phenomenon. Specifically, when politically influenced workers are "stuck" in adversely affected import-competing sectors, they are more likely to get short-term policy remediation in the form of higher tariffs. The more unequal the initial distribution of gains and losses from the magnitude of potential overshooting, the longer the induced policy distortion will persist.

In parallel with the political contribution model, the tariff formation function model (Findlay and Wellisz, 1982), the campaign contribution model (Magee *et al.*, 1989), the political support model (Rodrick, 1995), and the median voter model (Mayer, 1984) were developed and adopted to analyze agricultural policy formation. Other contributions to policymaking that have been emphasized more recently are institutions (Acemoglu and Robinson, 2006, 2012), limited access orders (North *et al.*, 2009), the role of constitutions (Persson and Tabellini, 2000), and electoral institutions (Besley and Persson, 2011).

4.2.2 *Loss aversion and trade policy interventions*

The G–H model hypothesizes that an individual's utility only depends on his or her consumption bundle, which meant it could not explain behavioral elements associated with the political economy dynamics behind trade protection (Dissanayake, 2014). Agents' preferences toward loss aversion and reference dependence are now being built into political contribution models (Freund and Özden, 2008; Tovar, 2009). Loss aversion refers to people's tendency to feel stronger about avoiding losses than acquiring gains, and losses reflect particular reference points. Freund and Özden (2008) explain why trade protection is given when the world price falls below a given reference price. Tovar (2009) incorporates individual preferences exhibiting loss aversion into the political objective function, and points out that an industry is more likely to organize and lobby the government if it suffers a loss.

During recent years, loss aversion has been built into analyses of government responses to market shocks. Anderson and Nelgen (2012c) set up loss aversion in quadratic rather than linear form, which is consistent with the conservative social welfare function in Corden (1997). They show that during upward price spike periods, developing countries alter their agricultural trade policies more than high-income countries, and vice versa during downward agricultural price shocks. Giordani *et al.* (2016) analyze the multiplier effect of food-exporting countries seeking to insulate the domestic market from the world market. Dissanayake (2014) presents a general equilibrium model that projects changes in trade restrictions irrespective of the lobbying behaviors of interested groups who make monetary contributions to the democratic government. Thennakoon (2015) follows Baldwin (1987) with a partial equilibrium model in which the government objective function is the weighted summation of consumer surplus, producer surplus, and tariff revenue, and uses loss aversion as in Freund and Özden (2008) and Tovar (2009) to analyze government responses to downward spikes in international prices. Loss aversion is also used by Fulton and Reynolds (2015) in considering the rice export system in a non-democratic country, Vietnam. They conclude that in such a setting, the elite could increase their political and economic power by restricting exports.

In this chapter, we document the effects of common interest groups on the government's trade policy formation process. The government's objective function is set with behavior features including reference dependence and loss aversion not only from a producer's perspective but also from that of consumers. China's cotton policy is shown to be consistent with the predictions of that theoretical model.

4.3 Geography, Politically Sensitive Products, and Preference

4.3.1 *Geography and politically sensitive products*

Policy pressure arises from policy preferences of self-interested agents. Economic actors can organize to influence government policy to their advantage because of the spatial distribution of economic endowments (Chase, 2015). Geography can sometimes shape individual's preferences, collective action, and aggregate preferences of the government if the endowment factor is located geographically in particular ways. Self-interest can be pursued by creating social unrest, sending petitions to the central government, or otherwise fighting for their rights. Regions with a high proportion of minorities in the total population can be highly sensitive politically, as can ones in which a product is concentrated in just one politically sensitive region. A formal definition of a politically sensitive product, drawing on Jean *et al.* (2011), could be as follows:

> A politically sensitive product is one whose output is produced using a specific endowment factor geographically located in a politically sensitive region, and the producers are vulnerable to changes in government policy affecting that product.

4.3.2 *Xinjiang*

The geographic location and the large share of Muslims in Xinjiang make it a politically sensitive region. The largest of China's administrative regions, Xinjiang borders eight countries — Mongolia, Russia, Kazakhstan, Kyrgyzstan, Tajikistan, Afghanistan, Pakistan, and India. It is located in the far northwest of China, and transportation links to the east through the central area of mainland China are weak. The shares of the total population of each province that is a minority are listed for 2014 in Table 4.1. Xinjiang ranks second only to Tibet out of the 26 provinces whose statistics are available, with 60% of its total population being Uyghur.

The higher the share of minorities in the province, the more they share common interests and preferences. The minorities are more likely to organize political groups to fight against local or central governments, or create social unrest to force the government to allocate benefits to them. In 2009, the biggest conflict between the Han and Uighur people occurred. In that social unrest, almost 200 people

Table 4.1 Share of minority in total population in each province in 2014.

Ranking	Province	%	Ranking	Province	%
1	Tibet	94.07	17	Hubei	4.34
2	Xinjiang	59.39	18	Hebei	4.31
3	Qinghai	45.51	19	Beijing	4.26
4	Guangxi	38.34	20	Tianjin	2.64
5	Guizhou	37.85	21	Fujian	1.67
6	Ningxia	34.53	22	Guangdong	1.42
7	Yunnan	33.41	23	Henan	1.22
8	Neimenggu	20.74	24	Zhejiang	0.85
9	Hainan	17.29	25	Shandong	0.86
10	Liaoning	16.02	26	Anhui	0.63
11	Hunan	10.21	27	Shanghai	0.6
12	Jilin	9.03	28	Shaanxi	0.49
13	Gansu	8.69	29	Jiangsu	0.33
14	Chongqing	6.42	30	Shanxi	0.29
15	Heilongjiang	5.02	31	Jiangxi	0.27
16	Sichuan	4.98	—	—	—

Notes: The unit of the value is percentage.

Data source: The sixth census of Chinese government and reports of the local government. http://tieba.baidu.com/p/3622083537.

were killed, 1721 people were injured, and 1000 people were arrested by the government. In 2014, there were nine social unrests related to the Xinjiang Uighur group whose number was much higher than other years.

4.3.3 *The role of cotton in Xinjiang*

Xinjiang's cotton sector plays an important role in China. The cotton yield in Xinjiang in 2009 was 123 kg per acre (M), which is one-quarter above the national average. Xinjiang's share of total production of cotton[2] in China was 30% in 2002, but then it sharply increased to 62.5% by 2015. Figure 4.2 illustrates the cotton production geography in China in 2012, when Xinjiang's share was 52%. Cotton production has become an important part of Xinjiang's economy. Cotton accounts for 65% of its crop sector and 1/3 of its total agricultural sector. More than 50% of people in Xinjiang are engaged in cotton production, and 35% of their income is from cotton on average — but that share was up to 60% in the cotton-intensive areas in 2009. For the local government, 15% of their fiscal income is from cotton production and related sectors. For some cotton-intensive production counties, the proportion of fiscal income peaks at more than 50%. The cotton sector also accounted for more than 17% of Xinjiang's GDP in 2013.

> "Cotton is intimately associated with land usage, ownership, employment, and Han immigration. It's all tied up."
>
> —Tom Cliff, a scholar at the Australian National University (20 February 2015).[3]

The Chinese government is more likely to protect cotton planters due to the important role of cotton in employment and income in Xinjiang. Social unrest and agricultural price shocks have a positive relationship, which has been tested recently by Bellemare (2014) and Arezki and Bruckner (2011). If a product is geographically concentrated in its production,[4] the Chinese government tends to protect the sector when considering major employment. Besides, those working as cotton planters are relatively unskilled. If the government does

---

[2] The average annual cotton production in China between 1995 and 2004 was 22, 319 [unit: thousand 480-pound bales], but it increased to a peak of 32,332 between 2005 and 2015.

[3] See http://www.businessinsider.com/r-top-china-cotton-producer-resists-reforms-in-restive-xinjiang-2015-2/?r=AU&IR=T.

[4] The coal sector in some European countries receives higher protection and government subsidy. The geographically concentrated industry is often a major employer in a town or city and involves a small number of towns or cities (Anderson, 1995b).

not protect the cotton sector, a higher unemployment rate may result and potentially lead to social and political unrest in Xinjiang. Maintaining social stability is an objective of China's cotton policies:

> "China's cotton policy is cognizant of social stability. They want to control rioting in the Xinjiang province, where most of the cotton is grown."
>
> —Elton Robinson (15 March, 2013)[5]

In short, cotton is a politically sensitive product whose production is geographically concentrated in Xinjiang province — a politically sensitive region.

4.3.4 *Cotton trade policy in China*

China is the world's largest cotton producer, consumer, and importer.[6] Table 4.2 shows China's net trade volumes between 2005 and 2015.

The Chinese government's trade policy has been largely focused on managing import flows to competing interests of consumers[7] and cotton farmers. A Sliding Scale Duty (SSD) system has been in place since 2005.

In China, its in-quota import volume includes regular quotas and additional quotas permitted by the SSD system. As illustrated in

Table 4.2 Cotton net import volume, 2005–2015.

Year	2005	2006	2007	2008	2009	2010	2011	2012	2013	2014	2015
Value	19212	10500	11468	6912	10880	11857	24478	20280	14096	8213	4800

Note: The unit of the value is (000) 480-pound bales.

Source: USDA-Foreign Agriculture Service.

---

[5] See "Chinese cotton policy- Social stability, not trade". *http://deltafarmpress.com/cotton/chinese-cotton-policy-social-stability-not-trade*.

[6] See Table 5.1 in Chapter 5, which gives more details of China's role in the international cotton market from 2000 to 2014.

[7] Cotton consumers are mills in the textile industry rather than citizens, because raw cotton is the intermediate input to produce clothes.

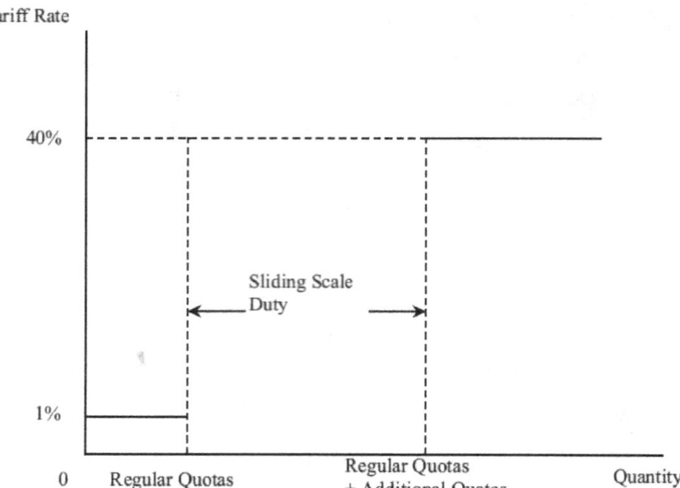

Fig. 4.2   China's actual TRQ system.
Source: Wang *et al.* (2014).

Fig. 4.2, within the regular import quota, the import tariff is very low at 1%. If the import exceeds the sum of the regular quota and additional quota, the tariff is taken to the highest level of 40%. If the import volume belongs to the additional quota, the government will implement an SSD to calculate the tariff rate under the SSD system, which is not allowed to be higher than 40%.

China's actual Tariff Rate Quota (TRQ) system shows that the tariff rate is fixed within the regular quotas. The fluctuations of tariff rates depend on the additional quotas' context.

Figure 4.3 gives the composition of cotton imports. The primary instruments determining China's cotton imports are import size, timing, and conditionality of quotas. Most of China's cotton imports are under the "Sliding Scale" quota (SSQ).

This chapter mostly focuses on the variation of the import tariff. It analyses how the tariff rate is calculated based on the SSD within the additional quotas range. The Chinese government introduced the SSD system in 2005 and has since adjusted it considerably.

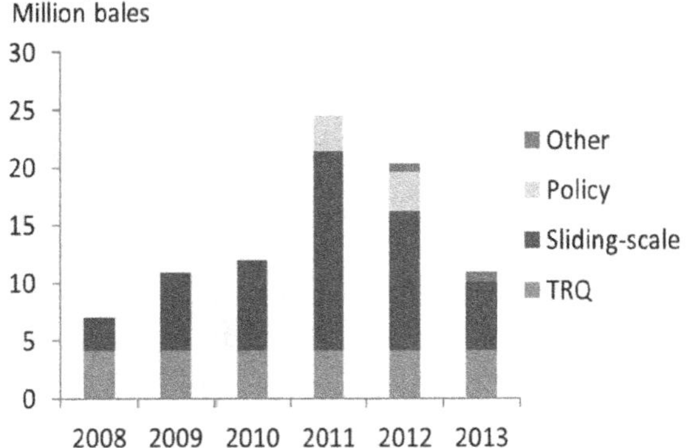

Fig. 4.3   China's cotton import composition during 2008–2013.

Notes: "Policy", e.g., imports by China National Cotton Reserves Corporation (CNCRC); "Other": imported at full 40% WTO bound tariff.

Source: MacDonald *et al.* (2015).

The SSD system is categorized into two stages (periods): During the first period (May 1, 2005–December 31, 2006), if the import price including Cost Insurance and Freight (CIF) was at or above a reference price $(\overline{P_t})^8$ set by the government, the tariff rate is 5% for imported cotton within the additional quotas. If the CIF price is higher than the reference price, the following formula was adopted to calculate cotton tariff rate:

$$T^I = \min(INT((P_t/CIF - 1)*1000 + 0.5)/1000, 0.4) \qquad (1)$$

where T^I is the import tariff rate in period one; CIF is the import price;[9] P_t is the value of $\overline{P_t}(1+0.05)$; and min is a minimum function

---

[8] The Chinese government sets the reference price (cost, insurance, and freight) for the lowest tariff on cotton imported under an SSQ (calendar year) (MacDonald *et al.*, 2015). The reference price was 10029 Yuan/Ton in 2005, 10746 Yuan/Ton in 2006, 11397 Yuan/Ton between 2007 and 2011, and 14000 yuan/Ton from 2012 to 2015.

[9] Under the SSD system, the Chinese government can import from any other cotton-exporting countries. These countries are competitive. In the empirical part, the CIF price is functioned as the world price.

indicating that the maximum import tariff value is 0.4. INT is an INT function to get the integer part of the value in the outer parentheses.

The second period covers a longer time (January 1, 2007–December 31, 2015) and the SSD for additional quota was managed by the government as follows. If the import price is at or above government's reference price $\overline{P_t}$, the tariff rate for import cotton was 0.57 Yuan per kg. If the import price is below the reference price, the import tariff is calculated using the following formula:

$$T^{II} = \min\left(INT\left(P'_t * CIF + \alpha * CIF - 1000 + 0.5\right) * 1000, 0.4\right)^{10} (2)$$

where T^{II} is the import tariff rates in period two; $P'_t = (1 + 0.05)\overline{P_t} - \alpha(\overline{P_t})^2$; α is a constant number whose value takes 2.526% from 2007 to 2011, 3.235% in 2012, and 2.908 in 2013, respectively.

From the SSD system, we can see that the import tariffs ranging from 1% to 40% are determined by the category of the imports and the year the cotton is imported. Wang *et al.* (2014) rewrite the above two formulas into an equivalent *ad valorem* tariff format, but it does not change the import tariff rules. In short, the tariff rate is inversely related to the international price.

4.4 Theoretical Framework

Cotton producers are almost always net sellers in the short term, which makes them different from staple food producers. The income effects due to a product's price change are not ambiguous for cotton planters: they gain when facing domestic market price increases, and vice versa.

This section presents a theoretical framework to be used in the applied empirical analysis in Section 4.5. Two cases are considered: a small open economy and a large open economy.

---

[10] See Wang *et al.* (2014).

4.4.1 *Model assumptions*[11]

Consider a small open economy populated by individuals with identical preferences. Individuals own different types of specific factors and labor endowments. All the agents have the following consumption preference characterized by loss aversion and reference dependence:

$$U = x_0 + \sum_1^n u_i(x_i) + \min\left(h\left(x_0 + \sum_1^n u_i(x_i) - \bar{U}\right), 0\right) \qquad (3)$$

where x_0 is a numeraire good produced only by labor with constant return to scale, and the input–output coefficient equals 1 ($x_0 = L_0$). The numeraire good could be defined as the import good or the export good. By definition, its domestic price and world price are equal to 1. Under a competitive labor market, the wage rate is equal to 1. x_i is consumption of good i, $i = 1, 2,\ldots, n$. All the normal goods require labor- and sector-specific inputs with fixed supply in the economy exhibiting constant returns to scale. While the specific factors are immobile across sectors, laborers have free mobility in the economy. With the wage rate equal to one, the returns to the specific factor owners depend only on the domestic market price p_i denoted by $\pi_i(p_i)$. The supply of good i is denoted by $y_i(p_i) = \pi_i'(p_i)$, which is an application of Hoteling's lemma.

Following Freund and Özden (2008), we introduce behavior features into consumer utility through a $h(-)$ function. The $h(-)$ function is called "gain–loss" utility[12] (Dissanayake, 2014), and its first derivative is positive[13] and second derivative is negative.[14] In other

---

[11] The author borrows some of the basic assumptions from Grossman and Helpman (1994) in the small open economy, and assumptions from Grossman and Helpman (1995) in the context of a large country. The difference between the two cases is whether the country can affect the international market price.

[12] The price of the numeraire goods is constant. Therefore, the utility function is linear in x_0 but not other normal goods.

[13] Indicating as $h'(\cdot) > 0$, which means the extent of loss an individual feels for having less than they are accustomed to.

[14] Indicating as $h''(\cdot) > 0$, which means the marginal increase is declining in the size of loss due to diminishing sensitivity to losses.

words, the gain–loss term is increasing the difference between the actual utility level and the reference utility level indicated by $\bar{U}$. $\bar{U}$ is an individual's reference utility derived from consuming a reference consumption bundle. The function takes a negative value when the actual utility is lower than the reference level, and zero otherwise. With the above preferences, an individual consumes $x_i = d_i(x_i)$ normal goods, $i = 1,2, \ldots, n$, where demand is the inverse of $U_i'^{-1}(p_i)$ and $x_0 = E - \sum_1^n p_i x_i$. The related indirect utility function is expressed as

$$W_i(p_i) = E - \sum_i p_i d_i(p_i) + \sum_{i=1}^n u_i(d_i(p_i))$$

$$+\min\left(h\left(E - \sum_i p_i d_i(p_i) + \sum_{i=1}^n u_i(d_i(p_i)) - \bar{U}\right), 0\right) \quad (4)$$

The utility equation could be rewritten as

$$W_i(p_i) = E + s(p_i) + \min\left(h\left(E + s(p_i) - \bar{U}\right), 0\right) \quad (5)$$

where $s(p_i) = \sum_{i=1}^n u_i(d_i(p_i)) - \sum_i p_i d_i(p_i)$ indicates the consumer surplus. If we denote the reference level of utility as $\bar{U} = \bar{E} + \overline{S(p)}$, then the above function (5) could be rearranged as:

$$W_i(p_i) = E + s(p_i) + \min\left(h\left(E + s(p_i) - \bar{E} - \overline{S(p)}\right), 0\right) \quad (6)$$

The wedge between the domestic market price (p_i) and the international market price (p_i^w) is t_i^s, created by the government's price-distorting policy. The relationship between the domestic market price and the world price is simply expressed as:

$$p_i = p_i^w + t_i^s \quad (7)$$

If $t_i^s > 0$, it means that the domestic market price is higher than that in the international market, indicating that the government imposes a tariff on imports or an export subsidy on exports. When $t_i^s < 0$, it means the domestic market price is lower than the world price, in which case imports are subsidized or exports are taxed.[15] As per the above assumption, the government only imposes trade distortions to manage the variations in the domestic price.

The assumed aim of the government is to maximize its objective by implementing price-distorting policies, with the ultimate objective being to stay in office and control the country's power. In the context of China, there is no formal lobby group to make money contributions to the government. However, interest groups can express their unwillingness or anger through, for example, creating social unrest. We model the government's political objective function as the summation of total political support from politically sensitive groups, and the aggregate welfare of the economy as the following linear function:

$$OFG = \sum_{i \in g} PS_i + \varphi \sum_{i=1}^{n} W\left(t_i^s\right), \varphi \geq 0 \tag{8}$$

where OFG is the objective function of the government; $\sum_{i \in g} PS_i$ is the political support from politically sensitive groups indicated by g; $W(t_i^s)$ is the aggregate social welfare; and φ represents the weight that the government puts on aggregate social welfare. The value of φ is a positive value. We propose that political support is a strictly monotonic increasing function with respect to the welfare of the politically sensitive group. Equivalently, the government's objective function could be rewritten as

$$\Omega = \sum_{i \in g} H\left(t_i^s\right) + \varphi \sum_{i=1}^{n} W\left(t_i^s\right), \varphi \geq 0 \tag{9}$$

In this model, the government of China considers politically sensitive areas which are geographically related to producing a specific product.

---

[15] The protected product could be import goods or export goods. In China, cotton is a type of net import agricultural product. The Chinese government imposes tariffs on import cotton to manage domestic market price.

The government would like to consider that region's welfare more than the welfare of other groups, which is expressed as follows:

$$\sum_{i \in g} H\left(t_i^s\right) = a_g l + a_g \sum_{i=1}^{n} t_i^s M_i\left(p_i\right) + \sum_{i \in g} \pi_i\left(p_i\right) + a_g \sum_{i=1}^{n} s_i\left(p_i\right) \quad (10)$$

where g in the third term is a set of politically sensitive groups which have the higher power to argue with the government, and a_g is the proportion of individuals in the total population who belong to the politically sensitive groups.

For the second term, the aggregate social welfare consists of four terms:

$$\sum_{i=1}^{n} W\left(t_i^s\right) = l + \sum_{i=1}^{n} t_i^s M_i\left(p_i\right) + \sum_{i=1}^{n} \pi_i\left(p_i\right) + \sum_{i=1}^{n} s_i\left(p_i\right) \quad (11)$$

where l is the total labor income (wage rate is one and total labor supply is l); $\sum_{i=1}^{n} t_i^s M_i(p_i)$ denotes total tariff revenue and $M_i(p_i)$ is the trade value for product i; $\sum_{i=1}^{n} \pi_i(p_i)$ is the total return for specific factors; and $\sum_{i=1}^{n} s_i(p_i)$ is the total consumer surplus.

The equilibrium optimal tariff rate can be solved by maximizing the government's objective function (Eq. (9)) with respect to the trade protection level (t_i^s):

$$t_i^s = \arg\max\left(\sum_{i \in g} H\left(t_i^s\right) + \varphi \sum_{i=1}^{n} W\left(t_i^s\right)\right) \quad (12)$$

4.4.2 *A small country model: Three scenarios*

Regarding the model assumptions, the individuals' preferences depend on the difference between the actual consumption and the reference consumption levels. Because of this, the form of the government objective function depends on the difference between the equilibrium domestic market price and the reference price set by the government authority. Therefore, three scenarios are considered in turn in analyzing the optimal trade policy for the government to maximize its object function: when the equilibrium price exactly equals, is lower than, or is higher than the reference price.

4.4.2.1 *The equilibrium domestic price equals the reference price*

When the domestic equilibrium market price equals the reference price, the individuals will have a utility function excluding the loss–gain term. The welfare of the politically sensitive groups and the aggregate social welfare are the same as Eqs. (10) and (11), respectively. Substituting the two equations into the government objective function (Eq. (9)), we get:

$$\Omega = \left[a_g l + a_g \sum_{i=1}^{n} t_i^s M_i(p_i) + \sum_{i \in g} \pi_i(p_i) + a_g \sum_{i=1}^{n} s_i(p_i) \right]$$
$$+ \varphi \left[l + \sum_{i=1}^{n} t_i^s M_i(p_i) + \sum_{i=1}^{n} \pi_i(p_i) + \sum_{i=1}^{n} s_i(p_i) \right] \tag{13}$$

Simplifying the above equation (13)

$$\Omega = \left(\varphi + a_g \right) l + \left(\varphi + a_g \right) \sum_{i=1}^{n} \left(t_i^s M_i(p_i) + s_i(p_i) \right)$$
$$+ \sum_{i=1}^{n} \left(\varphi + g_i \right) \pi_i(p_i) \tag{14}$$

Trying to choose the optimal trade protection vector (based on political support schedules) is equivalent to maximizing the objective function of the government with respect to protection level t_i^s, which is following the idea of equation (12). The first-order condition is given as the following equation (15) by using Roy's identity ($\frac{\partial s(p_i)}{\partial p_i} = -d_i(p_i)$) and Hotelling's lemma ($\pi_i'(p_i) = y_i(p_i)$), where $d_i(p_i)$ is domestic demand and $y_i(p_i)$ is the domestic supply for product i. Besides, the relationship between domestic market price and international market price (Eq. (5)) is applied here.

$$\left(\varphi + a_g \right) \left[-d_i(p_i) + t_i^s M_i'(p_i) + M_i(p_i) \right] + \left(\varphi + g_i \right) y_i(p_i) = 0 \tag{15}$$

The relationship between domestic demand, supply, and import is expressed as

$$M_i(p_i) - d_i(p_i) = -y_i(p_i) \tag{16}$$

Then, Eq. (15) can be expressed as:

$$\left(\varphi + a_g\right)\left[-y_i\left(p_i\right) + t_i^s M_i'\left(p_i\right)\right] + \left(\varphi + g_i\right)y_i\left(p_i\right) = 0 \qquad (17)$$

Rearranging the above equation, the optimal trade protection level is given by

$$t_i^s = \left[\frac{g_i - a_g}{\varphi + a_g}\right]\frac{y_i\left(p_i\right)}{-M_i'\left(p_i\right)} \qquad (18)$$

The solution can be rewritten as

$$\frac{t_i^s}{p_i} = \left[\frac{g_i - a_g}{\varphi + a_g}\right]\frac{z_i}{e_i} \qquad (19)$$

where $e = -\left(\Delta M_i(p_i)/M_i(p_i)\right)/\left(\Delta p_i/p_i\right) = \frac{\Delta M_i(p_i)}{\Delta p_i}\frac{p_i}{M_i(p_i)} = -M_i'\left(p_i\right)\frac{p_i}{M_i(p_i)}$ is the import demand or export supply elasticity of good i and $z_i = \frac{y_i(p_i)}{M_i(p_i)}$ is an equilibrium ratio of domestic output to imports (negative for exports). In the following, we change the form of the tariff to become *ad valorem*:[16]

$$\frac{t_i}{1 + t_i} = \left[\frac{g_i - a_g}{\varphi + a_g}\right]\frac{z_i}{e_i} \qquad (20)$$

This is the solution for the benchmark situation when the domestic equilibrium price equals the reference price. No loss aversion is created by an upward spike in the agricultural price for the consumers

---

[16] Because the domestic price ($p_i = p_i^w + t_i^s$) is known, we can get the trade distortion as $t_i^s = p_i - p_i^w$, then $\frac{t_i^s}{p_i} = \frac{p_i - p_i^w}{p_i}$. In the final step, the numerator and denominator are simultaneously divided by p_i^w:

$$\frac{t_i^s}{p_i} = \frac{p_i - p_i^w}{p_i} = \frac{\frac{p_i - p_i^w}{p_i^w}}{\frac{p_i}{p_i^w}} = \frac{\frac{p_i - p_i^w}{p_i^w}}{\frac{p_i - p_i^w + p_i^w}{p_i^w}} = \frac{\frac{p_i - p_i^w}{p_i^w}}{1 + \frac{p_i - p_i^w}{p_i^w}} = \frac{t_i}{1 + t_i}$$

or by a downward spike for the producers. From the above optimal protection, politically sensitive groups receive positive protection. This is because g_i is an indicator variable: If the group owns a specific factor to produce a politically sensitive product, the value equals one, and zero otherwise. The other effect of one specific product is the output-to-import ratio. If that one specific product accounts for a large share, the specific group has more power to gain from price distortions. The protection level is negatively related to the import demand elasticity. The other two variables are the weight on the aggregate social welfare, and the share of the population that belongs to the politically sensitive groups. In short, the predictions of the above optimal trade protection are as follows:

Benchmark results: *Politically sensitive groups receive positive protection. The protection level is positively related to the output–import ratio; negatively proportional to the share of the total population in the politically sensitive regions, the import demand elasticity, and the government's weight on the aggregate social welfare.*

4.4.2.2 *The equilibrium domestic price is below the reference price*

What should be the trade protection level when the equilibrium price is lower than the reference price? In this situation, the return of specific factors will be low due to the decrease in the output price. Therefore, the negative deviation of price from its reference price will result in further welfare loss for the producers through the loss aversion term if they produce that product.

Following the same argument as Freund and Özden (2008) and Dissanayake (2014), the producers pay more attention to the return of factor income than to changes in tariff revenue and consumer surplus. The other individuals, whose specific factors are not used to produce this product whose price decreases, are net buyers. The price decrease of this product will contribute to the positive gain of net indirect utility to consumers. However, the positive gain in the loss–gain function does not add additional utility gain.

Based on these arguments, the standard aggregate social welfare (Eq. (11)) becomes the following form:

$$\sum_{i=1}^{n} W\left(t_i^s\right) = l + \sum_{i=1}^{n} t_i^s M_i\left(p_i\right) + \sum_{i=1}^{n} \pi_i\left(p_i\right) + \sum_{i=1}^{n} s_i\left(p_i\right)$$
$$+ \min\left(-\sum_{i=1}^{n} a_i Nh\left(\frac{\overline{\pi_l} - \pi_i\left(p_i\right)}{\alpha_i N}\right), 0\right) \tag{21}$$

The first four terms are the same as Eq. (11), indicating total labor income, tariff revenue, total specific factor income, and consumer surplus. The last term in the above equation is the loss aversion part from producers whose specific factors experience return decreases, leading to negative social welfare. In the loss aversion term, α_i denotes the share of the population that owns one specific factor i and N is the total population.

Following the same logic, the welfare of the politically sensitive groups becomes

$$\sum_{i \in g} H\left(t_i^s\right) = \alpha_g l + \alpha_g \sum_{i=1}^{n} t_i^s M_i\left(p_i\right) + \alpha_g \sum_{i \in g} \pi_i\left(p_i\right)$$
$$+ \alpha_g \sum_{i=1}^{n} s_i\left(p_i\right) + \min\left(-\sum_{i \in g} a_i Nh\left(\frac{\overline{\pi_l} - \pi_i\left(p_i\right)}{\alpha_i N}\right), 0\right) \tag{22}$$

The only difference between Eqs. (22) and (10) is that the loss aversion term enters the welfare function, which is expressed as the last term in Eq. (22).

Therefore, we substitute Eqs. (21) and (22) into Eq. (9) and rearrange the equation as

$$\Omega = \left(\varphi + \alpha_g\right) l + \left(\varphi + \alpha_g\right) \sum_{i=1}^{n} \left(t_i^s M_i\left(p_i\right) + S_i\left(p_i\right)\right)$$
$$+ \sum_{i=1}^{n} \left(\varphi + g_i\right) \pi_i\left(p_i\right)$$
$$+ \min\left(-\sum_{i=1}^{n} \left(\varphi + g_i\right) a_i Nh\left(\frac{\overline{\pi_l} - \pi_i\left(p_i\right)}{\alpha_i N}\right), 0\right) \tag{23}$$

We maximize Ω with respect to t_i^s following the idea of Eq. (12), which yields the following first-order condition by using Roy's identity, Hotelling's lemma, and Eq. (7) again:

$$\left(\varphi + \alpha_g\right)\left[-d_i\left(p_i\right) + t_i^s M_i'\left(p_i\right) + M_i\left(p_i\right)\right] + \left(\varphi + g_i\right) y_i\left(p_i\right)$$

$$- \left(\varphi + g_i\right) a_i N h'\left(\frac{\overline{\pi_l} - \pi_i\left(p_i\right)}{\alpha_i N}\right) \frac{1}{\alpha_i N}\left(-y_i\left(p_i\right)\right) = 0 \qquad (24)$$

Solving this equation with respect to the optimal trade distortion and writing it in *ad valorem* form on good l gives

$$\frac{t_i}{1+t_i} = \left[\frac{g_i - a_g + \left(\varphi + g_i\right) h'\left(\cdot\right)}{\varphi + a_g}\right] \frac{z_i}{e_i} \qquad (25)$$

where e is import demand elasticity of good i or export supply, and z_i is an equilibrium ratio of domestic output to imports (negative for exports). Comparing the optimal protection level with Eq. (20), the only change is the term from the numerator $(\varphi + g_i) h'(\cdot)$. According to the characteristics of the loss aversion function, the first derivative is positive, illustrated as $h'(\cdot) > 0$, and then $(\varphi + g_i) h'(\cdot) > 0$. Thus, the optimal protection level is higher compared with the protection level when the equilibrium price equals the reference price. When trade protection is higher, the domestic market price must be higher than the world price. If the equilibrium domestic price goes lower than the reference price, the world price is lower than the reference price. Hence, the following Proposition holds:

Proposition 1: *When the world price is below its reference price, i.e., $p_i^w < \overline{p}_i$, the government introduces a higher distortion than the level of distortion when the world price is at the reference level.*

$$\left[\frac{g_i - a_g + \left(\varphi + g_i\right) h'\left(\cdot\right)}{\varphi + a_g}\right] \frac{z_i}{e_i} > \left[\frac{g_i - a_g}{\varphi + a_g}\right] \frac{z_i}{e_i} \qquad (26)$$

4.4.2.3 *The equilibrium domestic price is above the reference price*

If the equilibrium price goes above the reference price, producers gain. However, net buyers whose specific factors do not experience a price increase will lose. The loss aversion term enters the objective function of the government due to this loss of consumers' surplus. In the special case of cotton, the gain for producers dominates the situation. The difference between the gains in factor income and the loss in consumer surplus is positive for producers who are net sellers. In this scenario, the loss aversion term from consumers' perspective is added to the standard aggregate social welfare (Eq. (11)).

$$\sum_{i=1}^{n} W\left(t_i^s\right) = l + \sum_{i=1}^{n} t_i^s M_i\left(p_i\right) + \sum_{i=1}^{n} s_i\left(p_i\right) + \sum_{i=1}^{n} \pi_i\left(p_i\right)$$

$$+ \min\left(-\left(1-a_i\right) Nh\left(\frac{\overline{\sum_{l=1}^{n} t_i^s M_l} - \sum_{l=1}^{n} t_i^s M_l\left(p_i\right) + \overline{\sum_{l=1}^{n} s_l} - \sum_{i=1}^{n} s_i\left(p_i\right)}{N}\right), 0\right) \quad (27)$$

where a_i is the share of individuals who experience a price increase in the good they produce; $1 - a_i = \beta_i$ represents the share of individuals who are net buyers of the good that experiences a world price increase.

In this case, following the same logic, the welfare of the politically sensitive groups is as follows:

$$\sum_{i \in g} H\left(t_i^s\right) = \alpha_g l + \alpha_g \sum_{i=1}^{n} t_i^s M_i\left(p_i\right) + \alpha_g \sum_{i=1}^{n} s_i\left(p_i\right) + \sum_{i \in g} \pi_i\left(p_i\right)$$

$$+ \min\left(-\beta_i^g Nh\left(\frac{\overline{\sum_{l=1}^{n} t_i^s M_l} - \sum_{l=1}^{n} t_i^s M_l\left(p_i\right) + \overline{\sum_{l=1}^{n} s_l} - \sum_{i=1}^{n} s_i\left(p_i\right)}{N}\right), 0\right) \quad (28)$$

where β_i^g is the share of individuals who are net buyers of the good that experiences a world price increase in the politically sensitive groups. β_i^g is smaller or equal to β_i in the economy.

Substituting Eqs. (27) and (28) into Eq. (9), we get

$$\Omega = \left(\varphi + \alpha_g\right)l + \left(\varphi + a_g\right)\sum_{i=1}^{n}\left(t_i^s M_i\left(p_i\right) + s_i\left(p_i\right)\right)$$

$$+\sum_{i=1}^{n}\left(\varphi + g_i\right)\tau_i\left(p_i\right)$$

$$+ \min\left(-\left(\varphi\beta_i + \beta_i^g\right)Nh\left(\frac{\overline{\sum_{l=1}^{n}t_i^s M_l} - \overline{\sum_{l=1}^{n}t_i^s M_l\left(p_i\right)} + \overline{\sum_{l=1}^{n}s_l} - \sum_{i=1}^{n}s_i\left(p_i\right)}{N}\right), 0\right) \quad (29)$$

Applying Roy's identity, Hotelling's lemma, and Eq. (7), the first-order condition of Eq. (29) t_i^s is

$$\left(\varphi + a_g\right)\left[-d_i\left(p_i\right) + t_i^s M_i'\left(p_i\right) + M_i\left(p_i\right)\right] + \left(\varphi + g_i\right)y_i\left(p_i\right)$$

$$+ \left(\varphi\beta_i + \beta_i^g\right)Nh'\left(\cdot\right)\left[-y_i\left(p_i\right) + t_i^s M_i\left(p_i\right) + M_i\left(p_i\right)\right]\frac{1}{N} = 0 \quad (30)$$

Rearranging the above equation, we can solve the politically optimal trade protection:

$$t_i^s = \frac{\left[g_i - a_g - \left(\varphi\beta_i + \beta_i^g\right)h'\left(\cdot\right)\right]}{\left[\varphi + a_g + \left(\varphi\beta_i + \beta_i^g\right)h'\left(\cdot\right)\right]}\frac{y_i\left(p_i\right)}{-M_i'\left(p_i\right)} \quad (31)$$

Finally, we write the protection in *ad valorem* form on good i as

$$\frac{t_i}{1+t_i} = \left[\frac{g_i - a_g - \left(\varphi\beta_i + \beta_i^g\right)h'\left(\cdot\right)}{\varphi + a_g + \left(\varphi\beta_i + \beta_i^g\right)h'\left(\cdot\right)}\right]\frac{z_i}{e_i} \quad (32)$$

Compared with the benchmark protection level (Eq. (20)), the only different term entering the politically optimal solution is $\left(\varphi\beta_i + \beta_i^g\right)h'\left(\cdot\right)$, which takes a positive value according to the characteristics of the loss aversion function. The decrease of the numerator and the increase of the denominator lead to the ratio value decrease. Thus, the protection level is lower than in the scenario where the equilibrium domestic price equals the reference price. In addition, when the protection level is lower and the domestic market is lower than the reference price, the international market price must be lower than the reference price. Proposition 2 summarizes this conclusion as follows:

Proposition 2: *When the world price goes higher than the reference price, i.e., $p_i^w > \overline{p}_i$, the government introduces lower distortions than the level of distortion introduced when the world price is at its reference price.*

$$
\left[\frac{g_i - a_g - \left(\varphi\beta_i + \beta_i^g\right)h'(\cdot)}{\varphi + a_g + \left(\varphi\beta_i + \beta_i^{ps}\right)h'(\cdot)}\right]\frac{z_i}{e_i} < \left[\frac{g_i - a_g}{\varphi + a_g}\right]\frac{z_i}{e_i} \tag{33}
$$

4.4.3 *Do terms of trade effects matter?*

From the above general equilibrium model, we can predict the politically optimal tariff response in a small open economy to changes in the international market price. However, the politically optimal policies for a large open economy take into account a country's ability to influence its international terms of trade (Feenstra, 2016, p. 213). Broda *et al.* (2008) argue that market power explains more of the tariff variation than a commonly used political economy variable. Freund and Özden (2008) and Dissanayake (2014) ignore terms of trade. This subsection explores whether the above theoretical predictions for a small open economy are still relevant if terms of trade matter to the government.

We assume two countries exist and both have the power to affect the world price, but otherwise keep the same assumptions as in the small country case. The foreign country is indicated by *. The world price is expressed as p_i^w for product i. In order to simplify the calculation process, the relationship between the domestic market and international market is assumed to be $p_i = t_i p_i^w$ in the home country and $p_i^* = t_i^* p_i^w$ for the foreign country. If t_i and t_i^* are greater than one, it means the governments implement an import tariff or export subsidy. If t_i and t_i^* are less than one, it indicates an import subsidy or export tax. The political support functions are the same as in the small country case. The welfare of the politically sensitive groups is

$$\sum_{i \in g} H\left(t_i^s\right) = a_g l + a_g \sum_{i=1}^{n} r\left(t_i, p_i^w\right) + \sum_{i \in g} \Pi_i\left(t_i, p_i^w\right)$$
$$+ a_g \sum_{i=1}^{n} S\left(t_i, p_i^w\right) \tag{34}$$

where l continues to represent the total labor income. The remaining three terms are functions of trade protection and the world price. $r(t_i, p_i^w)$, $\Pi_i(t_i, p_i^w)$, and $S(t_i, p_i^w)$ indicate trade revenue, return for specific factors, and consumer surplus, respectively.

The aggregate welfare of the economy is expressed as the following equation whose four terms have the same meaning as Eq. (11). However, terms of trade effects are considered in this case:

$$\sum_{i=1}^{n} W\left(t_i^s\right) = l + \sum_{i=1}^{n} \Pi_i\left(t_i, p_i^w\right) + \sum_{i=1}^{n} r\left(t_i, p_i^w\right) + \sum_{i=1}^{n} S\left(t_i, p_i^w\right) \tag{35}$$

The objective function of the government does not change, which is the same as Eq. (9), and we continue to solve the politically optimal trade protection following the idea of Eq. (12).

4.4.3.1 *Equilibrium domestic price equals the reference price*

When the equilibrium domestic market price equals the reference price, the welfare change will not lead to any negative deviation from the target value. Because of this, the loss aversion term does not enter the government objective function, which is the same as scenario one of a small country case. Substituting the welfare of politically sensitive groups (Eq. (34)) and the aggregate social welfare (Eq. (35)) into government objective function (Eq. (9)) yields

$$\Omega = a_g l + a_g \sum_{i=1}^{n} r\left(t_i, p_i^w\right) + \sum_{i \in g} \Pi_i \left(t_i, p_i^w\right) + a_g \sum_{i=1}^{n} S\left(t_i, p_i^w\right)$$

$$+ \varphi l + \varphi \sum_{i=1}^{n} \Pi_i \left(t_i, p_i^w\right) + \varphi \sum_{i=1}^{n} r\left(t_i, p_i^w\right) + \varphi \sum_{i=1}^{n} S\left(t_i, p_i^w\right) \tag{36}$$

The trade revenue function $(r(t_i, p_i^w))$ is known as the product of trade quantity and tariff rate:

$$r\left(t_i, p_i^w\right) = \sum_{i=1} (t_i - 1) p_i^w \left[d_i \left(t_i, p_i^w\right) - \frac{1}{N} y_i \left(t_i, p_i^w\right) \right] \tag{37}$$

Substituting Eq. (37) into Eq. (36) and rearranging the function gives

$$\Omega = \left(a_g + \varphi\right) l + \left(\varphi + g_i\right) \sum_{1}^{n} \Pi_i \left(t_i, p_i^w\right)$$

$$+ \left(a_g + \varphi\right) \left\{ \sum_{i=1} (t_i - 1) p_i^w \left[d_i \left(t_i, p_i^w\right) - \frac{1}{N} y_i \left(t_i, p_i^w\right) \right] \right.$$

$$\left. + \sum_{i=1}^{n} S\left(t_i, p_i^w\right) \right\} \tag{38}$$

Maximizing the objective function of the government with respect to t_i provides the first-order condition:

$$\left(\varphi + g_i\right) y_i p_i^w + \left(\varphi + g_i\right) y_i t_i p_{i1}^w + \left(a_g + \varphi\right)$$

$$\left[g_i M_i \left(t_i, p_i^w\right) + (t_i - 1) p_{i1}^w M_i \left(t_i, p_i^w\right) + (t_i - 1) p_i^w M_i' p_i^w \right.$$

$$\left. + (t_i - 1) p_i^w t_i M_i' p_{i1}^w - d_i \left(t_i, p_i^w\right) p_i^w - d_i \left(t_i, p_i^w\right) t_i p_{i1}^w \right] = 0 \tag{39}$$

Equation (39) is simplified as

$$(g_i - a_g)\left(p_i^w + t_i p_{i1}^w\right) y_i + \left(\varphi + a_g\right)$$

$$\left[(t_i - 1) p_i^w \left(p_i^w + t_i p_{i1}^w\right) M_i' - p_{i1}^w M_i \left(t_i, p_i^w\right) \right] = 0 \tag{40}$$

In the two large countries' case, the terms of trade effects matter for the variance of trade distortions. Based on the world market-clearing condition, one obtains the following equation:

$$M_i\left(t_i, p_i^w\right) + M_i^*\left(t_i^*, p_i^w\right) = 0 \quad i = 1, 2, \ldots, n. \tag{41}$$

The partial derivative of the world price with respect to the home country's trade policy is expressed as

$$p_{i1}^w = \frac{\partial p_i^w}{\partial t_i} = -\frac{M_i' p_i^w}{M_i' t_i + M_i'^* t_i^*} \tag{42}$$

The politically optimal trade protection is solved by substituting Eqs. (41) and (42) into Eq. (40) to get

$$\left(t_i - 1\right) = \frac{\left(g_i - a_g\right)}{\left(\varphi + a_g\right)} \frac{y_i}{p_i^w\left(-M_i'\right)} + \frac{1}{e_i^*} \quad \text{for } i = 1, 2, \ldots, n \tag{43}$$

The above solution is the maximized political target function regarding the protection level for the home country.[17] $e_i^* = \frac{p_i^w M_i'^* t_i^*}{M_i^*}$ is the elasticity of the foreign country's export supply. Compared with the small country case, the only difference is the terms of trade effect expressed as $\frac{1}{e_i^*}$.

4.4.3.2 *The equilibrium domestic price is lower than the reference price*

When the domestic equilibrium price goes below the reference price, producers will experience a loss. Following the same idea as in scenario two in the small country case, the loss aversion part for the producers will enter the objective function of the government.

---

[17] The unilateral trade policy for the foreign country could be derived through the same method expressed as $(t_i^* - 1) = -\frac{\left(g_i^* - a_g^*\right)}{\left(\varphi^* + a_g^*\right)} \frac{y_i^*}{p_i^w M_i^*} + \frac{1}{e_i}$. The resulting structure is the same as for the home country.

The other individuals whose specific factors are not used to produce this product are net buyers. The price decrease of this product will contribute to a positive gain of net indirect utility. However, the positive gain in the loss–gain function does not add additional utility gain to consumers. In this case, the aggregate social welfare becomes

$$\varphi \sum_{i=1}^{n} W\left(t_i^s\right) = \varphi l + \varphi \sum_{i=1}^{n} \Pi_i\left(t_i, p_i^w\right) + \varphi \sum_{i=1}^{n} r\left(t_i, p_i^w\right)$$

$$+ \varphi \sum_{i=1}^{n} S\left(t_i, p_i^w\right) + \min\left(-\sum_{i=1}^{n} a_i N h\left(\frac{\overline{\pi_I} - \Pi_i\left(t_i, p_i^w\right)}{a_i N}\right), 0\right) \quad (44)$$

The welfare of the politically sensitive groups will be expressed as follows:

$$\sum_{i \in g} H\left(t_i^s\right) = a_g l + a_g \sum_{i=1}^{n} r\left(t_i, p_i^w\right) + \sum_{i \in g} \Pi_i\left(t_i, p_i^w\right) + a_g \sum_{i=1}^{n} S\left(t_i, p_i^w\right)$$

$$+ \min\left(-\sum_{i \in g} a_i N h\left(\frac{\overline{\pi_I} - \Pi_i\left(t_i, p_i^w\right)}{a_i N}\right), 0\right) \quad (45)$$

Plugging Eqs. (44) and (45) into the government objective function (Eq. (9)) gives

$$\Omega = a_g l + a_g \sum_{i=1}^{n} r\left(t_i, p_i^w\right) + \sum_{i \in g} \Pi_i\left(t_i, p_i^w\right) + a_g \sum_{i=1}^{n} S\left(t_i, p_i^w\right)$$

$$+ \min\left(-\sum_{i \in g} a_i N h\left(\frac{\overline{\pi_I} - \Pi_i\left(t_i, p_i^w\right)}{a_i N}\right), 0\right)$$

$$+ \varphi l + \varphi \sum_{i=1}^{n} \Pi_i\left(t_i, p_i^w\right) + \varphi \sum_{i=1}^{n} r\left(t_i, p_i^w\right)$$

$$+ \varphi \sum_{i=1}^{n} S\left(t_i, p_i^w\right) + \min\left(-\sum_{i=1}^{n} a_i N h\left(\frac{\overline{\pi_I} - \Pi_i\left(t_i, p_i^w\right)}{a_i N}\right), 0\right) \quad (46)$$

Substituting the tariff revenue equation (37) into (46) yields

$$
\Omega = \left(a_g + \varphi\right)l + \left(\varphi + g_i\right)\sum_1^n \Pi_i\left(t_i, p_i^w\right) + \left(a_g + \varphi\right)
$$

$$
\times \left\{ \sum_{i=1}^n \left(t_i - 1\right) p_i^w \left[d_i\left(t_i, p_i^w\right) - \frac{1}{N} y_i\left(t_i, p_i^w\right)\right] + \sum_{i=1}^n S\left(t_i, p_i^w\right)\right\}
$$

$$
+ \min\left(-\sum_{i=1}^n \left(\varphi + g_i\right) a_i N h\left(\frac{\overline{\pi_I} - \sum_i^n \Pi_i\left(t_i, p_i^w\right)}{a_i N}\right), 0\right) \tag{47}
$$

Maximizing the above function with respect to t_i gives the first-order condition as follows:

$$
\left(\varphi + ps_i\right) y_i p_i^w + \left(\varphi + ps_i\right) y_i t_i p_{i1}^w + \left(a_g + \varphi\right)
$$

$$
\times \left[p_i^w M_i\left(t_i, p_i^w\right) + \left(t_i - 1\right) p_{i1}^w M_i\left(t_i, p_i^w\right) + \left(t_i - 1\right) p_i^w M_i' p_i^w\right.
$$

$$
\left. + \left(t_i - 1\right) p_i^w t_i M_i' p_{i1}^w - d_i\left(t_i, p_i^w\right) p_i^w - d_i\left(t_i, p_i^w\right) t_i p_{i1}^w \right]
$$

$$
- \left(\varphi + ps_i\right) a_i N h'\left(\cdot\right) \frac{1}{a_i N}\left(-y_i p_i^w - y_i t_i p_{i1}^w\right) = 0 \tag{48}
$$

Solving the optimal trade protection level by applying Eqs. (41) and (42) gives

$$
\left(t_i - 1\right) = \frac{\left[g_i - a_g + \left(\varphi + g_i\right) h'\left(\cdot\right)\right]}{\left[a_g + \varphi\right]} \frac{y_i}{p_i^w\left(-M_i'\right)} + \frac{1}{e_i^*} \tag{49}
$$

Comparing Eq. (49) with Eq. (43), the only change is the term in the numerator $\left(\varphi + g_i\right) h'\left(\cdot\right)$, which is positive according to the characteristics of the loss aversion function. This means the protection level is higher compared with the protection level when the equilibrium price equals the reference price. When trade protection is higher, the domestic market price must be higher than the world price.

If the equilibrium domestic price goes lower than the reference price, the world price is lower than the reference price. Therefore, we can conclude that the terms of trade do not change the result of Proposition 1, which could be expressed as follows:

$$\left\{ \frac{[g_i - a_g + (\varphi + g_i)h'(\cdot)]}{[a_g + \varphi]} \frac{y_i}{p_i^w(-M_i')} + \frac{1}{e_i^*} \right\}$$
$$> \left\{ \frac{(g_i - a_g)}{(\varphi + a_g)} \frac{y_i}{p_i^w(-M_i')} + \frac{1}{e_i^*} \right\} \tag{50}$$

4.4.3.3 *The equilibrium domestic price is higher than the reference price*

If the equilibrium price is higher than the reference price, producers gain. Following the arguments of Freund and Özden (2008), when the producers own one specific factor and the product experiences an increase of price, the return dominates the loss aversion term for producers. However, the net buyers whose specific factors do not experience price increases will have loss aversion effects. The loss aversion term enters the government objective function due to loss of consumers' surplus. In this scenario, adding the loss aversion term from consumers' perspective means the standard aggregate social welfare (Eq. (11)) becomes

$$\varphi \sum_{i=1}^{n} W\left(t_i^s\right) = \varphi l + \varphi \sum_{i=1}^{n} \Pi_i\left(t_i, p_i^w\right) + \varphi \sum_{i=1}^{n} r\left(t_i, p_i^w\right) + \varphi \sum_{i=1}^{n} S\left(t_i, p_i^w\right)$$
$$+ \min\left(-\varphi \beta_i N h \left(\frac{\overline{\sum_{l=1}^{n} r\left(t_i, p_i^w\right) - \sum_{l=1}^{n} r\left(t_i, p_i^w\right)} + \sum_{l=1}^{n} S\left(t_i, p_i^w\right) - \sum_{i=1}^{n} S\left(t_i, p_i^w\right)}{N} \right), 0 \right) \tag{51}$$

Following the same idea, the welfare of the politically sensitive groups becomes

$$\sum_{i\in g} H\left(t_i^s\right) = a_g l + a_g \sum_{i=1}^{n} r\left(t_i, p_i^w\right) + \sum_{i\in g} \Pi_i\left(t_i, p_i^w\right)$$

$$+ a_g \sum_{i=1}^{n} S\left(t_i, p_i^w\right)$$

$$+ \min\left(-\beta_i^g Nh\left(\frac{ \overline{ \sum_{l=1}^{n} r\left(t_i, p_i^w\right) } - \sum_{l=1}^{n} r\left(t_i, p_i^w\right) + \overline{ \sum_{l=1}^{n} S\left(t_i, p_i^w\right) } - \sum_{i=1}^{n} S\left(t_i, p_i^w\right) }{ N } \right), 0 \right)$$

$$\tag{52}$$

Substituting the above two Eqs. (51) and (52) into the government objective function (Eq. (9)) yields

$$\Omega = \varphi l + \varphi \sum_{i=1}^{n} \Pi_i\left(t_i, p_i^w\right) + \varphi \sum_{i=1}^{n} r\left(t_i, p_i^w\right) + \varphi \sum_{i=1}^{n} S\left(t_i, p_i^w\right)$$

$$+ \min\left(-\varphi\beta_i Nh\left(\frac{ \overline{ \sum_{l=1}^{n} r\left(t_i, p_i^w\right) } - \sum_{l=1}^{n} r\left(t_i, p_i^w\right) + \overline{ \sum_{l=1}^{n} S\left(t_i, p_i^w\right) } - \sum_{i=1}^{n} S\left(t_i, p_i^w\right) }{ N } \right), 0 \right)$$

$$+ a_g l + a_g \sum_{i=1}^{n} r\left(t_i, p_i^w\right) + \sum_{i\in g} \Pi_i\left(t_i, p_i^w\right) + a_g \sum_{i=1}^{n} S\left(t_i, p_i^w\right)$$

$$+ \min\left(-\beta_i^g Nh\left(\frac{ \overline{ \sum_{l=1}^{n} r\left(t_i, p_i^w\right) } - \sum_{l=1}^{n} r\left(t_i, p_i^w\right) + \overline{ \sum_{l=1}^{n} S\left(t_i, p_i^w\right) } - \sum_{i=1}^{n} S\left(t_i, p_i^w\right) }{ N } \right), 0 \right)$$

$$\tag{53}$$

From tariff revenue equation (37), Eq. (53) could be rewritten as

$$\Omega = \left(a_g + \varphi\right)l + \left(\varphi + g_i\right)\sum_1^n \Pi_i\left(t_i, p_i^w\right) + \left(a_{ps} + \varphi\right)$$

$$\times \left\{\sum_{i=1}\left(t_i - 1\right) p_i^w\left[d_i\left(t_i, p_i^w\right) - \frac{1}{N} y_i\left(t_i, p_i^w\right)\right] + \sum_{i=1}^n S\left(t_i, p_i^w\right)\right\}$$

$$+ \min\left(-\left(\varphi\beta_i + \beta_i^g\right) Nh\left(\frac{\begin{array}{c}\sum_{l=1}^n r\left(t_i, p_i^w\right) - \sum_{i=1}^n\left(t_i - 1\right) \\ p_i^w\left[d_i\left(t_i, p_i^w\right) - \frac{1}{N} y_i\left(t_i, p_i^w\right)\right] \\ + \sum_{l=1}^n S\left(t_i, p_i^w\right) - \sum_{i=1}^n S\left(t_i, p_i^w\right)\end{array}}{N}\right), 0\right)$$

(54)

We can get the following first-order condition by using Roy's identity, Hotelling's lemma, and the relationship between the domestic market price and the international market price:

$$\left(\varphi + g_i\right) y_i p_i^w + \left(\varphi + g_i\right) y_i t_i p_{i1}^w + \left(a_g + \varphi\right)\left[p_i^w M_i\left(t_i, p_i^w\right)\right.$$

$$+ \left(t_i - 1\right) p_{i1}^w M_i\left(t_i, p_i^w\right) + \left(t_i - 1\right) p_i^w M_i' p_i^w + \left(t_i - 1\right) p_i^w t_i M_i' p_{i1}^w$$

$$\left. - d_i\left(t_i, p_i^w\right) p_i^w - d_i\left(t_i p_i^w\right) t_i p_{i1}^w\right] - \left(\varphi\beta_i + \beta_i^g\right) Nh'(\cdot)$$

$$\times \left[-p_i^w M_i\left(t_i, p_i^w\right) - \left(t_i - 1\right) p_{i1}^w M_i\left(t_i, p_i^w\right) - \left(t_i - 1\right) p_i^w M_i' p_i^w\right.$$

$$\left. - \left(t_i - 1\right) p_i^w t_i M_i' p_{i1}^w + d_i\left(t_i, p_i^w\right) p_i^w + d_i\left(t_i, p_i^w\right) t_i p_{i1}^w\right]\frac{1}{N} = 0$$

(55)

Rearranging the above function, we can get the optimal protection level by applying Eqs. (41) and (42):

$$\left(t_i - 1\right) = \frac{\left[g_i - a_g - \left(\varphi\beta_i + \beta_i^g\right)h'(\cdot)\right]}{\left[a_g + \varphi + \left(\varphi\beta_i + \beta_i^g\right)h'(\cdot)\right]}\frac{y_i}{p_i^w\left(-M_i'\right)} + \frac{1}{e_i^*}$$

(56)

Compared with case one in a large country, the term $(\varphi\beta_i + \beta_i^g)h'(\cdot)$, which takes a positive value according to the characteristics of the loss aversion function, enters the numerator and denominator of the politically optimal trade policy. The decrease of the numerator and the increase of the denominator lead to the ratio value decreasing. Thus, the protection level is lower than in the scenario when the equilibrium domestic price equals the reference price. In addition, when the protection level is lower and the domestic market price is lower than the reference price, the international market price must be lower than the reference price. Finally, we can conclude that the large country model does not change the theoretical prediction of Proposition 2 when considering the terms of trade effect. This is illustrated in the following inequality equation:

$$\left\{ \frac{\left[g_i - a_g - \left(\varphi\beta_i + \beta_i^g\right)h'(\cdot)\right]}{\left[a_g + \varphi + \left(\varphi\beta_i + \beta_i^g\right)h'(\cdot)\right]} \frac{y_i}{p_i^w(-M_i')} + \frac{1}{e_i^*} \right\}$$
$$< \left\{ \frac{(g_i - a_g)}{(\varphi + a_g)} \frac{y_i}{p_i^w(-M_i')} + \frac{1}{e_i^*} \right\} \tag{57}$$

4.5 Empirical Test

In this section, we investigate the cotton protection pattern in China for consistency with our theoretical model predictions. The cotton sector provides an ideal experiment to analyze trade policy formation motives of the government. First, as illustrated in Section 4.3.4, China's imports account for virtually all of China's cotton trade activity. Second, cotton is a special agricultural product, and it makes up a relatively smaller share of expenditure for poor producers, and in most cases, they are net sellers (Martin, 2009). This is exactly the same as our model assumptions. During price spike periods, the income of the cotton producer dominates the producers' "loss–gain" utility.

The Chinese government has set a cotton reference price[18] in each year from 2005 to 2015. For this reason, we do not have to estimate the reference price. This helps us test the effects of loss aversion and reference dependence on trade policy formation more accurately. Finally, the cotton producers in Xinjiang benefit when the government increases the tariff (helped by the fact that the Chinese government subsidizes domestic transportation of cotton delivered from Xinjiang to southeast regions of the country).

4.5.1 *Data sources*

In the empirical part, we apply monthly, seasonal, and annual frequency data to run the empirical model. The monthly data cover 132 months from May 2005 to December 2015. Trade protection is measured by NRA[19] calculated using the domestic cotton price and the international market price. China's cotton monthly prices are mainly collected from the China Cotton Almanac from January 2005 to October 2014, and the data from November 2014 to December 2015 are compiled from the website of China Cotton.[20] The international cotton price is from the National Cotton Council of America (NCCA) between January 2005 and December 2015. To measure the world cotton price in Renminbi (RMB), the monthly exchange rate data are collected from the Board of Governors of the Federal Reserve System (2005–2015).[21] The reference price is the annual value set by the Chinese government at the beginning of each year. The reference price does not stick to a fixed value, and it increased from 10,029 Yuan/Ton in 2005 to 12,935 Yuan/Ton in 2015. Concerning seasonal fluctuations, we aggregate the monthly data to the seasonal level and add the harvest cycle as the control variable

---

[18] Freund and Özden (2008) set the reference price as the average of the world price during a particular period.

[19] See "Measuring distortions to agricultural incentives, Revisited" Anderson *et al.* (2008) for more details of NRA indicator.

[20] See *http://www.cncotton.com/*.

[21] See *http://www.federalreserve.gov/releases/h10/hist/default1989.htm*.

measured by sin(·) and cos(·) functions. These data are created by combining the value of π and code numbers of the domestic price series. As a robustness check, a seasonal dummy variable is also applied to control for the production cycles. Meanwhile, in order to test for it being a politically sensitive product, the annual panel data method is implemented by covering 11 agricultural products and the NRA data are from Anderson and Nelgen (2013).

4.5.2 *The effects of political sensitivity on cotton trade protection*

One prediction is that a politically sensitive product receives a higher protection level relative to non-politically sensitive products. Trade protection for different types of products is measured by NRA. The products include cotton, poultry, fruits, rice, sugar, soybean, and wheat. Figure 4.4 illustrates the extent of trade protection for six agricultural products excluding sugar. Cotton trade protection is higher compared with other agricultural products, according to

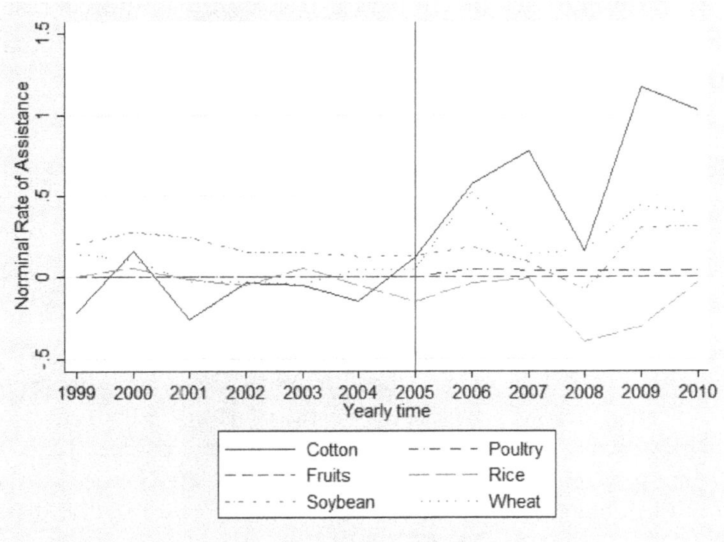

Fig. 4.4   Cotton compared with other agricultural products' trade protection.

Fig. 4.4.[22] The policy transfers from taxing to subsidizing the cotton sector could be explained by the theoretical model because of cotton's role as a politically sensitive product. The increasing trend of cotton protection provides a lower bound in the case of China's access to the WTO, which depresses the extent of agricultural distortions.[23]

In order to confirm the theoretical prediction and the role of politically sensitive products, we add two dummy variables to represent cotton and sugar. Table 4.3 reports the empirical regression results between politically sensitive product dummies and the change of border trade protection by applying panel data. From column 1–5, the effect of politically sensitive cotton on the changes of its trade protection is positive and statistically significant at the 1% level. Year dummy and product dummy variables are all controlled in the five models. Cotton receives 0.023 point higher trade protection measured by NRA when controlling the international price as reported in column 1. When adding the self-sufficiency ratio (column 2), production value in GDP (column 3), consumption value in total agriculture (column 4), and production value in total agriculture (column 5) into the regression as control variables, the effect size is still around 0.01 and statistically significant. Unlike for cotton, the empirical results do not show any significant effect of the dummy variable for sugar from columns 1 to 5 reported in Table 4.3.

4.5.3 *The effects of loss aversion on cotton trade protection*

This section empirically tests the effects of loss aversion and reference dependence on the variations of trade restriction in the China cotton

---

[22] Sugar receives higher protection than cotton or other agricultural products. However, sugar is not geographically produced in one or a few regions. In the empirical part, we test whether sugar is a politically sensitive product. However, that hypobook is not supported by the econometrics (see Table 4.3).

[23] For a further argument later, the loss aversion effect may be affected by WTO restrictions. In the seasonal and monthly data regressions, we just apply the data starting from 2005. Thus, the WTO effect is a constant dummy variable. Thus, we could exclude the confound effect of WTO.

Table 4.3 Effect of politically sensitive products on the changes of protection level.

Variables	Δ Protection level (1)	Δ Protection level (2)	Δ Protection level (3)	Δ Protection level (4)	Δ Protection level (5)
Dummy variable for cotton	0.023***	0.011**	0.011**	0.010*	0.010**
	(0.003)	(0.005)	(0.005)	(0.005)	(0.005)
Dummy variable for sugar	0.012	0.007	0.005	0.006	0.007
	(0.091)	(0.005)	(0.007)	(0.007)	(0.006)
Δ ln (world price)	−0.392***	−0.406***	−0.415***	−0.397***	−0.390***
	(0.091)	(0.069)	(0.083)	(0.087)	(0.080)
Δ self-sufficiency ratio		−0.451	−0.458	−0.493	−0.468
		(0.290)	(0.286)	(0.306)	(0.291)
Δ production value in GDP			0.408	0.930	1.515*
			(0.677)	(0.587)	(0.791)
Δ consumption value in total agriculture				−0.474	—
				(0.477)	—
Δ production value in total agriculture					−0.944
					(0.662)
Constant	0.034***	0.037***	0.035***	0.034***	0.032**
	(0.012)	(0.012)	(0.012)	(0.013)	(0.013)
Year dummy	Yes	Yes	Yes	Yes	Yes
Product dummy	Yes	Yes	Yes	Yes	Yes
Observations	300	300	300	300	300
No. of products	11	11	11	11	11
Adj. R^2	0.484	0.484	0.484	0.484	0.484

Notes: (1) Robust standard errors are reported in the parentheses; (2) *significant at 10%; **significant at 5%; ***significant at 1%.

sector, both when the world price is lower than the reference price and when it is higher than reference price.

4.5.3.1 *Visual figure illustration*

The relationship between cotton trade protection, the international market price, and the reference price is illustrated in Fig. 4.5. The

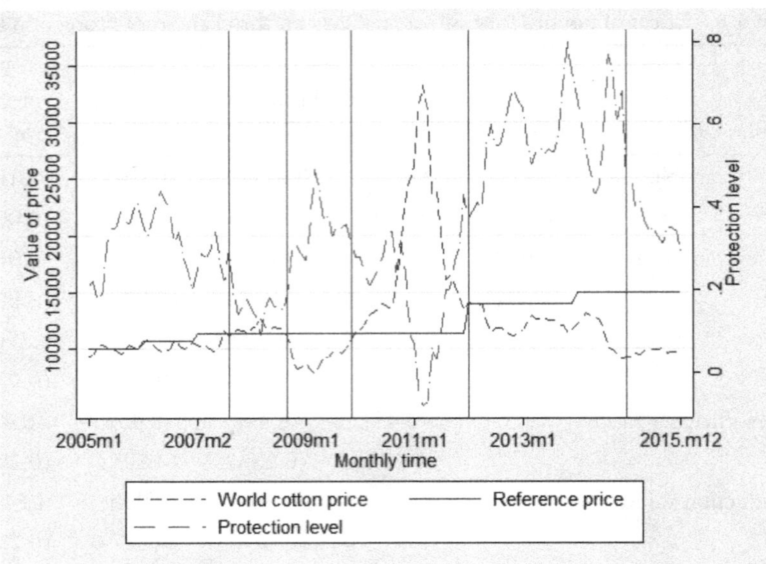

Fig. 4.5   Relationships between world price, reference price, and trade protection.

author divides the period into six, depending on the level of world price compared with the reference price level. The dotted line indicates the international market price and the dashed line represents the level of China cotton trade protection. The horizontal line is the domestic reference price set by the government. When the world price is lower than the reference price, the trade protection level is higher, and when the world price is higher than that of the reference price, the cotton protection level is lower. This is consistent with the theoretical model predictions summarized as Propositions 1 and 2.

When world price is lower and trade protection is higher, compensating protection is triggered for producers (Freund and Özden, 2008). One interesting finding is in the last period. When the world price continues to decrease, cotton protection sharply decreases despite being outside the compensation period. That government behavior could be explained by diminishing sensitivity to loss.[24]

---

[24] Diminishing sensitivity means that the marginal value of gains and loss decreases with their size.

The continuous decrease in the world price leads producers to adjust their planting and investing behaviors. Finally, they accept the loss phenomenon due to the further decrease of the world price. According to the production data, total production of cotton in China decreased from 30 million 480-pound bales in 2014 to 23.8 million a year later.

Visually, Fig. 4.5 illustrates the theoretical predictions quite well between the trade protection level, the reference price, and the world price due to loss aversion effects. However, that does not tell us if the effects of loss aversion and reference dependence are statistically significant. In the following, the correlation is tested using the whole sample and subsamples.

4.5.3.2 *Correlation confirmation*

Table 4.4 reports the correlation and significance level between trade protection and the world price contingent on the reference and the magnitude of loss aversion effects from consumers and producers during world price upward spike and downward spike periods, respectively. The relationship between the international market price and cotton trade protection level should be negatively correlated. The correlation is calculated from the full sample and subsample separately. Based on the calculation of the full sample, the correlation between China cotton protection and the international market price is -0.4237, which is significantly different from zero at a 1% significant level. When applying the first half sample and the other later half sample to the robustness checks for correlation, the absolute value of

Table 4.4 Correlation between cotton trade protection and international market price.

Correlation size	Sample chosen
-0.4237***	Full sample
-0.6646***	Subsample between Jan 2005 and May 2010
-0.7397***	Subsample between Jun 2010 and Dec 2015

Notes: ***Significantly different from zero at 1% significant level.

the coefficient increases from 0.4237 to 0.6646 for the first half subsample and then further to 0.7397 for the second half subsample. Both of the coefficients, calculated from two subsamples, are negative and statistically significant at a 1% level. According to the coefficient equality test, the calculated z-value is equal to −0.995. Thus, we could not reject the null hypobook referring to the two-subsample coefficients as equal.

4.5.3.3 *Empirical regression test*

In order to further confirm the loss aversion effect on the fluctuations of trade protection level, a complementary econometric regression method is adopted in this part. Table 4.5 reports the regression results by applying monthly time series data. Because the time series for China cotton price, the international market price, and cotton

Table 4.5 World price changes on changes of cotton protection level.

Variables	Δ Protection level (1)	Δ Protection level (2)	Δ Protection level (3)	Δ Protection level (4)	Δ Protection level (5)
Δ ln (world cotton price)	−0.654***	−0.654***	−1.347***	−3.129***	−2.378***
	(0.062)	(0.093)	(0.039)	(0.370)	(0.4429)
Δ ln (China cotton price)			1.416***	1.393***	1.381***
			(0.054)	(0.052)	(0.053)
Δ ln (square of world cotton price)				0.093***	0.051**
				(0.019)	(0.024)
Δ ln (world cotton price) × Dummy (world price higher or lower than reference price)					0.096
					(0.049)
Constant	0.001	0.001	−0.000	−0.000	−0.000
	(0.004)	(0.004)	(0.001)	(0.001)	(0.001)
Observations	131	131	131	131	131
Adj. R^2	0.456	0.456	0.973	0.979	0.980

Notes: (1) (Robust) standard errors are reported in the parentheses; (2) **significant at 5%; ***significant at 1%.

trade protection are not stationary,[25] first differences of the three indicators are calculated. Column 1 reveals that a 10% decrease of the international cotton price leads to the cotton trade protection level increasing by 0.065 points measured by NRA without controlling other variables. The effect of world price changes on China's cotton trade protection does not change when the robust standard error is applied in column 2. In columns 3 and 4, China's cotton price and the square term of world cotton price are added as control variables. The effect size increases by adding more control variables. The price comparison between world price and reference may have heterogeneous effects when the world price is higher or lower than the reference price. The interaction term is added into regression as shown in column 5. The result shows that when the world price is higher or lower than the reference price, the result does not change greatly.

4.5.3.4 *Do production cycles and time trends matter?*

Agricultural price and trade protection may be affected by production cycles and a time trend. Therefore, we use the seasonal data to test the effect by controlling the harvest cycles through $\sin(\cdot)$ and $\cos(\cdot)$ functions reported in column 1 (see Table 4.6). Though harvest production cycles have no significant effect on trade protection fluctuations, they add to the effect between changes of world price and changes of cotton trade protection levels in China. The time trend is added as a control variable reported in column 2. Quantitatively, a 10% fall in the international market price leads to an improvement of 1.1 points in the Nominal Rate of Assistance (NRA) and the effect is statistically significantly at the 99% confidence level. Following a traditional approach to control production cycles, a seasonal dummy variable is added to the model in column 3 and time trends are further controlled in column 4. The effect size of the world price changes on cotton protection changes is 0.11 with a negative sign and it is

---

[25] According to ADF tests, MacKinnon approximate *p*-values for the trade protection and the international cotton price variables are 0.2389 and 0.5535, respectively.

Table 4.6   Changes of the world price and changes of protection level.

Variables	Δ Protection level (1)	Δ Protection level (2)	Δ Protection level (3)	Δ Protection level (4)
Δ ln (world cotton price)	–11.328***	–11.311***	–10.968***	–10.906***
	(1.396)	(1.463)	(1.241)	(1.289)
Δ ln (China cotton price)	1.023***	1.000***	1.009***	0.988***
	(0.179)	(0.178)	(0.181)	(1.812)
Δ ln (square of world cotton price)	0.531***	0.530***	0.514***	0.511***
	(0.066)	(0.069)	(0.058)	(0.061)
Δ cos(·)	0.020	0.023	—	—
	(0.019)	(0.020)	—	—
Δ sin(·)	–0.007	–0.007	—	—
	(0.022)	(0.022)	—	—
Seasonal dummy	—	—	0.003	0.002
			(0.007)	(0.007)
Constant	–0.000	0.014	–0.006	0.004
	(0.001)	(0.015)	(0.198)	(0.021)
Time trend	—	Yes	—	Yes
Observations	43	43	43	43
Adj. R^2	0.757	0.076	0.752	0.756

Notes: (1) (Robust) standard errors are reported in the parentheses; (2) ***significant at 1%.

statistically significant at 1% when the international market price decreases by 1%.

Compared with the effect reported in Table 4.5, the effect size in Table 4.6 sharply increases by applying seasonal data. This increase could potentially be explained by the sticky and delayed changes of trade policy in response to international market price: the Chinese government prefers to adjust trade policy across seasons rather than altering trade policy promptly and sharply each month.

4.6 Conclusions

Research to explain variances in trade restrictions in non-democratic and developing countries is rare. Based on Freund and Özden's (2008) model, this chapter provides a political support model characterized by spatial dimensions of interest group politics to explain changes in trade restrictions in China. The results explain trade distortion fluctuations from two perspectives. On the one hand, politically sensitive groups receive greater protection. On the other hand, the target of the government's changing trade distortions is to stabilize the domestic market by insulating it from short-term fluctuations in the international market. This behavior of the government could be explained by introducing loss aversion and reference dependence into the government's objective function. The government reduces protection when the world price is higher than the target reference price if the loss aversion for consumers is large enough, and it reduces the protection level when the world price is lower than the target reference price if the loss aversion for producers is large enough.

In order to uncover the ambiguous effects of terms of trade on trade policy jointly with loss aversion, the model is extended to a large country case. The results show that terms of trade effects do matter for the trade protection level. However, the effect of loss aversion is independent of the terms of trade effects.

Finally, we apply our theoretical model to the cotton sector in China, and the empirical results favorably explain the puzzling cotton protection policy in China between 2005 and 2015. Cotton is a politically sensitive product which is produced intensively in Xinjiang province. Consistent with the model predictions, cotton gets positive protection that is much higher than that provided for other agricultural products. For a small extension, the changing format of cotton protection compared with other agricultural products could explain the changing variance of protection within a country over time. The short-term fluctuations of cotton protection could be explained by adding the feature of loss aversion. In order to insulate the domestic market from the international market, cotton trade protection is higher when the world price is lower than the reference price due to producers' loss aversion, and the cotton protection level is lower when the international market price is higher than the reference price due to loss aversion of consumers. The Chinese government evidently uses trade restrictions to balance income redistribution between cotton producers and consumers.

Political Economy of Trade and Storage Policy Coordination, and the Role of Domestic Public Storage in the World Market

5.1 Introduction

During world price fluctuation periods, the Chinese government not only applies trade distortions but also carries out a domestic storage policy to stabilize domestic agricultural prices by "buying low and selling high". Between 2010 and 2014, the Chinese government bought up a large amount of domestic cotton at high support prices and stored it in their government reserve. The other perplexing phenomenon is that the government still stores some imports in the official reserve. Cotton storage in China has climbed to 65,632 million 480lb bales[1] which is equivalent to more than 55% of the world's

---

[1] See footnote 4 in Chapter 1.

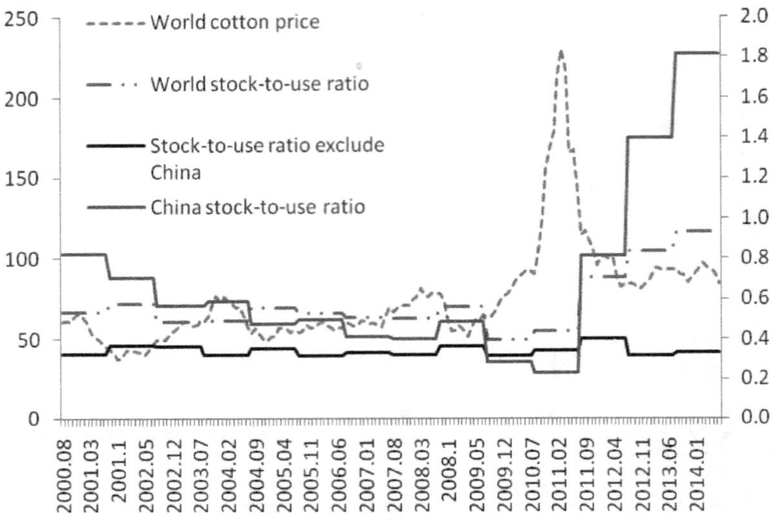

Fig. 5.1   SUR and world cotton price.

annual production in 2014.[2] China, as the largest player in the world, could potentially have a significant effect on the international cotton market, particularly on the world cotton price.

World cotton prices in 2010 reached the highest level in the past half-century. However, the world cotton price promptly returned to a more normal level (dot line in Fig. 5.1) from 2011. Compared to the stock-to-use ratios (SUR),[3] including world SUR, the ROW cotton SUR, and SUR of China, China dominated fluctuations in the world cotton market from 2011 to 2014. The mass increase of the world SUR is driven by soaring cotton storage in China.

MacDonald *et al.* (2015) note that a future release of China's large stockpile of cotton could depress the world cotton price to a considerable degree, consistent with research by Wiggins and

---

[2] The year in this chapter refers to crop year instead of calendar year. The world cotton production, consumption, import, export, and storage are all measured in crop year periods. Thus, we adopt the world cotton price in crop years as well.

[3] $SUR = \frac{\text{Ending stock}}{\text{(Mill use+export)}}$. The SUR is a convenient measure of supply and demand interrelationships of cotton. It indicates the level of carryover cotton stock as a percentage of the total demand, which equals total use plus export.

Keats (2009). According to Wright and Williams (1982), Wright (2002, 2011), and Gouel (2012, 2013), a low level of storage is one of the main factors that can contribute to spikes in agricultural product prices when the market receives a production shortfall or an unexpected surge in demand.

Previous research mostly focuses on the welfare effects of trade and storage policies. However, no research, to the best of the author's knowledge, tries to explore the government's motivations in the context of trade policy and domestic storage policy coordination. In this chapter, we develop a partial equilibrium model which is consistent with the political economy model in Chapter 4 but also incorporates domestic storage to explore government motivations. The results show that domestic storage policy strengthens price stabilization motivation in the context of trade policy, and can reinforce price-insulating trade policy. However, the effects of the two price stabilization instruments on the international market price are in opposite directions.[4] That is, the domestic public storage policy has a stabilization effect on the international market price, whereas trade policy actions add to international price fluctuations.

Previous research on the price-stabilizing effect of domestic storage on the international market price has been very limited compared to that of trade distortions. Thus, the effects of domestic storage on the world market are empirically tested in this chapter, again using China cotton as a case study. We ask "what if" China did not increase its cotton storage during 2011–2014. A vector autoregression (VAR) model is used to model the effects of China's cotton storage on the world cotton market. The exogenous behavior of the Chinese cotton storage policy provides an ideal experiment to apply counterfactual data to simulate the effects of China's cotton storage on the world cotton market.

---

[4] Trade policy intervention functions as the border instrument to insulate domestic market price from the international market price by controlling trade volumes. Storage policy is a domestic policy to stabilize the domestic market price by smoothing the quantity of the agricultural product available for purchase on the domestic market.

The VAR econometrics reveals that in the case of cotton during 2011–2014, China as a large player in the global market was able to stabilize to a non-trivial extent the international price of cotton through altering its public stockpile. The dynamic mechanism is more complex than static partial equilibrium model predictions. The relationships indicate that the sale of cotton from China's stockpile would depress world production and suppress storage by the ROW, resulting in a subsequent increase of the world market price and a decline in world cotton consumption.

The structure of this chapter is as follows: Section 5.2 reviews pertinent literature; Section 5.3 assesses the political incentives for cotton storage and the role of China's cotton in the international market; the VAR model is set out in Section 5.4 and the model qualifications are tested in Section 5.5; the counterfactual effects of China's public cotton storage is simulated in Section 5.6; and Section 5.7 concludes.

5.2 Literature Review

Numerous articles document the effects of agricultural trade insulation policies during upward price spike periods (Abbott, 2011; Anderson, 2012, 2013; Martin and Anderson, 2011, 2012; Anderson and Nelgen, 2012a; Ivanic and Martin, 2014; Anderson and Thennakoon, 2015) and also downward price periods (Thennakoon and Anderson, 2015). Importing countries feel susceptible to sudden world price spikes, especially if dominant exporters have a history of limiting their exports at such times (Bouët and Laborde Debucquet, 2012). When a shock in the world food market drives up prices, unilateral actions by exporting countries accentuate that price rise (Giordani *et al.*, 2016). If importing countries respond by lowering their import restrictions, that pushes the international price even higher (Anderson and Nelgen, 2012b; Thennakoon and Anderson, 2015). In this environment, domestic public storage can play a complementary role by "buying low and selling high". Of course, the government's intervention could crowd out private storage agents because of political uncertainty and perhaps regulations limiting profit from arbitrage (Wright and William, 1982; Tschirley and Jayne, 2010). Before the 2008 food crisis, the world SUR reached a low level and a decline in SUR indeed contributed to food price volatility in 2008 (Wright, 2009). The relationship between grain stocks and price spikes analyzed by Wiggins and Keats (2009), however, found that Chinese grain stocks were largely irrelevant to global markets because they were meant to insure against domestic shortage.

Cotton price spikes are different from staple food price spikes. The price elasticity of demand for cotton is much higher than that of staple food in the short term. Consumers can continue to wear their current clothes and do not tend to buy cotton products during price peaks at the highest level, so cotton price spikes have few direct adverse impacts on the incomes of the poor (Martin, 2009). Meanwhile, cotton producers enjoy price spikes, as most of them are net cotton sellers.

5.3 Government Motivations behind Domestic Storage Policies

This chapter explores the role of public storage policy in contributing to the government's objective of stabilizing the domestic market price, and explains the political motivations in the context of border and domestic policy coordination. It then provides evidence of the effects of domestic storage on the world cotton market price during a cotton price-declining period, going beyond the analysis of upward price spike periods.

5.3.1 *Model framework and predictions*

5.3.1.1 *Model setting*

Consider a partial equilibrium model of a global agricultural market. There are two countries, Home and Foreign, and Foreign is indicated by an asterisk "*". The demand of each country is set as linear and identical: $d(P_t) = a - P_t$ and $d(P_t^*) = a - P_t^*$. P_t and P_t^* denote the agricultural product prices. Consumer surplus functions are defined as

$CS_t = \int_{P_t}^{a}(a - P_t)d_{P_t}$ and $CS_t^* = \int_{P_t^*}^{a}(a - P_t^*)d_{P_t^*}$ for each country. In terms of production of the agricultural product, we assume that the good is produced with a specific factor in both countries. The input–output coefficient is constant with the value of one. Let x_t and x_t^* denote the quantity of specific factor used to produce this good, and assume the production functions are inelastic. For the owners of the specific factors, their return could be calculated as the products of domestic price and the volume of output, written as $P_t x_t$ and $P_t^* x_t^*$ for importing and exporting countries. Home is always in a position to import from the foreign country. In this case, the two random outputs should satisfy the production and deficit conditions, and trade positions always hold such that $x_t^* > x_t$.

During world market price downward (upward) spikes, the importer will impose higher (lower) import tariffs, τ_t. Conversely, the agricultural-exporting country at such times tends to decrease (raise) exporter barriers τ_t^*. We assume that the government implements border distortions, so the wedge between domestic market price and world price is $P_t = P_t^w + \tau_t$ and $P_t^* = P_t^w + \tau_t^*$, where P_t^w is defined as the world market price. In addition, we assume that the home country adopts a domestic storage policy as well, aiming to stabilize the domestic market through "buying low and selling high". The single representative speculative agent is assumed to be risk neutral and to act competitively. Storage goods quantity, Z_{t-1}, is allowed to be transferred from one period to the next. The domestic market-clearing condition could be expressed as

$$Z_{t-1} + x_t + M_t = d\left(P_t\right) + Z_t \tag{1}$$

where M_t represents the quantity of imports of the agricultural product.

5.3.1.2 *World price equilibrium determination*

The world market price is determined by the international market-clearing condition. The total world demand for the agricultural product includes the total consumption in both countries plus the storage demand in the home country in period t. The total world demand can be written as

$$D_t^{total} = d(P_t) + Z_t + d(P_t^*) = \left[a - (P_t^w + \tau_t)\right] + Z_t + \left[a - (P_t^w + \tau_t^*)\right]$$

(2)

The total world supply in period t covers production in both countries and the storage in the previous period $t - 1$ in the home country.

$$S_t^{total} = S_t + S_t^* = x_t + Z_{t-1} + x_t^*$$

(3)

Therefore, the world market-clearing condition is

$$x_t + Z_{t-1} + x_t^* = \left[a - (P_t^w + \tau_t)\right] + Z_t + \left[a - (P_t^w + \tau_t^*)\right]$$

(4)

We can get the equilibrium international market price by solving the above equation:

$$P_t^w = a - \frac{\tau_t + \tau_t^*}{2} - \frac{x_t + x_t^*}{2} + \frac{\Delta Z_t}{2}$$

(5)

where $\Delta Z_t = Z_t - Z_{t-1}$.

In the absence of a storage policy, the world price would be

$$P_t^{w\prime} = a - \frac{\tau_t + \tau_t^*}{2} - \frac{x_t + x_t^*}{2}$$

(6)

In a situation of free trade, the world price would be

$$P_t^f = a - \frac{x_t + x_t^*}{2}$$

(7)

Given the relationship between the domestic market price and the world market price, equilibrium domestic market prices for home and foreign countries are

$$\begin{cases} P_t = P_t^w + \tau_t = a + \dfrac{\tau_t - \tau_t^*}{2} - \dfrac{x_t + x_t^*}{2} + \dfrac{\Delta Z_t}{2} \\[4mm] P_t^* = P_t^w + \tau_t^* = a + \dfrac{\tau_t^* - \tau_t}{2} - \dfrac{x_t + x_t^*}{2} + \dfrac{\Delta Z_t}{2} \end{cases} \tag{8}$$

5.3.1.3 *Trade volumes and revenue*

The import trade volume is the difference between demand and supply in the home country:

$$M_t = d\left(P_t\right) + Z_t - x_t - Z_{t-1} = \dfrac{\tau_t^* - \tau_t}{2} + \dfrac{x_t^* - x_t}{2} + \dfrac{\Delta Z_t}{2} \tag{9}$$

The import revenue for the home country is given by

$$\tau_t M_t = \tau_t \left(\dfrac{\tau_t^* - \tau_t}{2} + \dfrac{x_t^* - x_t}{2} + \dfrac{\Delta Z_t}{2} \right) \tag{10}$$

For the foreign country, the export trade volume is calculated as

$$E_t = d\left(P_t^*\right) - x_t^* = \dfrac{\tau_t - \tau_t^*}{2} + \dfrac{x_t - x_t^*}{2} - \dfrac{\Delta Z_t}{2} \tag{11}$$

The import and export volumes are the same in absolute value, but they have opposite signs.

The export subsidy or tax of the foreign country is given by

$$\tau_t^* E_t = \tau_t^* \left(\dfrac{\tau_t - \tau_t^*}{2} + \dfrac{x_t - x_t^*}{2} - \dfrac{\Delta Z_t}{2} \right) \tag{12}$$

Accordingly, in the absence of the home country's storage policy, the trade volume would be

$$M_t' = \dfrac{\tau_t^* - \tau_t}{2} + \dfrac{x_t^* - x_t}{2} \tag{13}$$

Free trade volume would be

$$M_t^f = \frac{x_t^* - x_t}{2} \tag{14}$$

5.3.1.4 *Government objective function*

We model the government's preference as an aggregate of welfare, which is able to account for the various economic and political motivations. The government is trying to maximize the social welfare function, including producer's surplus, consumer's surplus, storage policy revenue, and tariff revenue. In Chapter 4, we incorporate loss aversion into the government's objective function and the results indicate that the government has the incentive to stabilize domestic agricultural price by insulating domestic market from the international market. Therefore, in this chapter, a quadratic term in the domestic price is added into the government objective function characterizing the preference for price stability (Anderson and Nelgen, 2012c; Gouel, 2016), which is consistent with the political model in Chapter 4. The government objective functions are defined as functions of trade policies and home country's storage policy by

$$\begin{cases} W_t = \int_{P_t}^{a} (a - P_t) d_{P_t} + P_t x_t + \tau_t M_t + \delta \Delta Z_t - \dfrac{\lambda}{2} (P_t - \bar{P})^2 \\ W_t^* = \int_{P_t^*}^{a} (a - P_t^*) d_{P_t^*} + P_t^* x_t^* + \tau_t^* E_t - \dfrac{\lambda}{2} (P_t - \bar{P})^2 \end{cases} \tag{15}$$

The first three terms represent consumer surplus, producer revenue, and trade revenue or cost. $\delta \Delta Z_t$ is the cost or revenue of changing domestic storage policy in static equilibrium. $\lambda \geq 0$ is a parameter characterizing the preference for price stability (Gouel, 2016). Consistent with Chapter 4, the government tries to stabilize the domestic market by undertaking trade policies that are related not just to high agricultural prices but also to downward price spikes. The parameter of preference for price stability (λ) does not go to infinity,[5] making $P_t = \bar{P}$. $\bar{P}$ is the reference price, which is defined the same as in Chapter 4. The reference price is a target price, set by the government, around which policymakers want the price to be stabilized.

5.3.1.5 *Politically optimal storage and trade policy*

Before analyzing the static Nash equilibrium, we first explore the motivations of trade policies and domestic storage policy in responding to fluctuations in the international market price. To get the politically optimal trade and storage policies, we maximize government objective functions (W_t and W_t^*) with respect to trade policies and storage policy separately. Therefore, the politically optimal policies are given by taking the first-order conditions of Eq. (15):

$$\begin{cases} \tau_t = \dfrac{(1+\lambda)\tau_t^* + (1+\lambda)x_t^* + (\lambda-1)x_t + (3-\lambda)\Delta Z_t + 2(\lambda\bar{P} - a\lambda)}{(3+\lambda)} \\[2em] \Delta Z_t = \dfrac{(\lambda-1)\tau_t^* + (\lambda-1)x_t^* + (\lambda+1)x_t + (3-\lambda)\tau_t + 2(\lambda\bar{P} - a\lambda + 2\delta)}{(\lambda-1)} \\[2em] \tau_t^* = \dfrac{2\lambda\bar{P} - 2a\lambda + (1+\lambda)\tau_t - (1+\lambda)\Delta Z_t + (1+\lambda)x_t - (1-\lambda)x_t^*}{3+\lambda} \end{cases}$$

$$\tag{16}$$

In order to get the economic and political motivations of each policy, optimal trade policies are rewritten as functions of free trade price and reference price. Home country's optimal storage policy is written as a function of the reference price and the international market price in the context of trade distortions. From Eqs. (5) and (6), the politically optimal policies are as follows:

---

[5] First, the higher preference of agricultural price stabilization leads to higher social welfare cost. Second, the stabilized price results in a revenue loss for the storage representative speculative agent.

$$
\left\{
\begin{aligned}
\tau_t &= \frac{\overbrace{\lambda\left(\overline{P}-P_t^{w}\right)}^{\text{Price smoothing by trade policy}} - \overbrace{\left(x_t - a - 2\Delta Z_t + P_t^{w}\right)}^{\text{Market power}}}{\left(2+\lambda\right)} \\[2ex]
\Delta Z_t &= \frac{\overbrace{\lambda\left(\overline{P}-P_t^{w'}\right)}^{\text{Price smoothing by storage policy}} + \overbrace{(2-\lambda)\tau_t}^{\text{Trade policy effect}} + \overbrace{2\delta}^{\text{Storage revenue}} + \overbrace{\left(x_t - a + P_t^{w'}\right)}^{\text{Market power}}}{\dfrac{\left(\lambda-1\right)}{2}} \\[2ex]
\tau_t^{*} &= \frac{\overbrace{\lambda\left(\overline{P}-P_t^{w}\right)}^{\text{Price smoothing by trade policy}} - \overbrace{\left(x_t^{*} - a + P_t^{w}\right)}^{\text{Market power}}}{\left(2+\lambda\right)}
\end{aligned}
\right.
\tag{17}
$$

The trade policy in each country could be divided into two terms. The first term is the government price-smoothing motivation by insulating the domestic market from the international market. This term is the price adjustment welfare cost of the world price deviating from the reference price. The importer tends to apply import tax (subsidy) and the exporter is more likely to apply an export subsidy (tax) when the world price is lower (higher) than the reference price. The second term represents the country's market power, which allows an optimal trade policy to maximize social welfare. The difference between home country and the foreign country is that storage power goes into determining the politically optimal trade policy. The home country could apply a storage policy to affect its terms of trade, which could benefit the home country's social welfare. The politically optimal storage policy includes four terms. The first term represents the price-smoothing motivation in the context of trade policy, which allows a complimentary trade policy to help stabilize the domestic market price. The second term is the trade policy effect incorporating the price stabilization preference. The storage revenue motivation and market power effect are expressed in the last two terms separately.

5.3.1.6 *The Nash equilibrium*

We write the interior Nash equilibrium and express all results as a function of the free trade price and volume, so that the best policy responses are expressed as follows. One optimal policy depends on the best responses from the other two optimal policies.

$$\begin{cases} \tau_t = 2\dfrac{\lambda\left(\bar{P}-P_t^f\right)+M_t^f}{(3+\lambda)} + \dfrac{(\lambda+1)}{(3+\lambda)}\tau_t^* + \dfrac{(3-\lambda)}{(3+\lambda)}\Delta Z_t \\[2ex] \Delta Z_t = 2\dfrac{\lambda\left(\bar{P}-P_t^f\right)-M_t^f+2\delta}{(\lambda-1)} + \tau_t^* + \dfrac{(3-\lambda)}{(\lambda-1)}\tau_t \\[2ex] \tau_t^* = 2\dfrac{\lambda\left(\bar{P}-P_t^f\right)-M_t^f}{(3+\lambda)} + \dfrac{(1+\lambda)}{(3+\lambda)}\tau_t - \dfrac{(1+\lambda)}{(3+\lambda)}\Delta Z_t \end{cases} \tag{18}$$

In order to solve the Nash equilibrium, we write the above three equations in a system of equations as follows:

$$\begin{cases} \tau_t - \dfrac{(\lambda+1)}{(3+\lambda)}\tau_t^* - \dfrac{(3-\lambda)}{(3+\lambda)}\Delta Z_t = 2\dfrac{\lambda\left(\bar{P}-P_t^f\right)+M_t^f}{(3+\lambda)} \\[2ex] \dfrac{(\lambda-3)}{(\lambda-1)}\tau_t - \tau_t^* + \Delta Z_t = 2\dfrac{\lambda\left(\bar{P}-P_t^f\right)-M_t^f+2\delta}{(\lambda-1)} \\[2ex] -\dfrac{(1+\lambda)}{(3+\lambda)}\tau_t + \tau_t^* + \dfrac{(1+\lambda)}{(3+\lambda)}\Delta Z_t = 2\dfrac{\lambda\left(\bar{P}-P_t^f\right)-M_t^f}{(3+\lambda)} \end{cases} \tag{19}$$

We can solve these equations in terms of τ_t, τ_t^*, and ΔZ_t. The three government policies are endogenously determined and expressed as functions of other exogenous parameters, including λ, δ, $\bar{P}$, P_t^f, and M_t^f:

$$
\left\{
\begin{array}{l}
\tau_t^{N} = \dfrac{\lambda^2 M_t^{f} - 2M_t^{f} - \lambda^2 P_t^{f} + \lambda^2 \overline{P} + 4\delta - \lambda\delta - \lambda^2\delta}{\lambda^2 + 2\lambda - 4} \\[4mm]
\tau_t^{*N} = \dfrac{2M_t^{f} - 2\lambda M_t^{f} + \lambda^2 M_t^{f} + 4\lambda P_t^{f} - \lambda^2 P_t^{f} - 4\lambda\overline{P} + \lambda^2\overline{P} - \lambda\delta - \lambda^2\delta}{\lambda^2 + 2\lambda - 4} \\[4mm]
\Delta Z_t^{N} = \dfrac{-2\lambda M_t^{f} - 4\lambda P_t^{f} - 2\lambda^2 P_t^{f} + 4\lambda\overline{P} + 2\lambda^2\overline{P} + 4\delta + 2\lambda\delta}{\lambda^2 + 2\lambda - 4}
\end{array}
\right.
$$

$$\tag{20}$$

The above Nash equilibrium solution helps us to get the Nash international market price as a function of price stabilization preferences and storage revenue.

5.3.1.7 *The Nash equilibrium international market price*

Based on the interior Nash equilibrium solutions, the Nash equilibrium price is a function of Nash equilibrium trade policies in both countries and the Nash equilibrium storage policy in the home country. The relationship is expressed as

$$
P_N^{w} = P_t^{f} - \frac{\tau_t^{N} + \tau_t^{*N}}{2} + \frac{\Delta_t^{N}}{2} \tag{21}
$$

Substituting the Nash equilibrium solutions for τ_t^{N}, τ_t^{*N}, and ΔZ_t^{N} into the above Nash equilibrium, international market price reveals that the effects of trade policies and home country's storage policy are in opposite directions. The Nash equilibrium world price is rearranged and simplified as

$$
P_N^{w} = P_t^{f} - \frac{\tau_t^{N} + \tau_t^{*N}}{2} + \frac{\Delta Z_t^{N}}{2} = P_t^{f} + \frac{\left(\lambda^2 + 2\lambda\right)\delta + 4\lambda\left(\overline{P} - P_t^{f}\right) - \lambda^2 M_t^{f}}{\lambda^2 + 2\lambda - 4}
$$

$$\tag{22}$$

The Nash equilibrium price consists of two terms. The first term is the benchmark free trade market price in the absence of trade policies and storage policy. The additional term is the effect of storage revenue and the price stabilization preference on the international market price. With the above equation, we will exploit the effects of a price stabilization preference and storage revenue on the international market price in the context of border and domestic storage policy coordination.

According to theoretical predictions by Gouel (2016), a higher price stabilization preference leads to a higher Nash international market price, and a large country contributes more than small countries (Giordani *et al.*, 2016). However, in the context of domestic and border policy coordination, the Nash equilibrium international market price is a nonlinear function of the price stabilization preference parameter, and the international market price is not monotonically increasing with respect to trade distortions.

Figure 5.2 illustrates the changes in the international market price with respect to the preference for price stabilization and storage revenue. Panels A1 and A2 show the response of international price to the changes in price stabilization preference (λ) and the effect of storage revenue (δ) when the free trade price is lower than the reference price. Panel A1 shows the reaction of the change of the international market price under lower trade volume conditions, and the results in Panel A2 reveal the responses when the trade volume is higher. The international market price responses are in Panel B1 (under lower trade volume) and Panel B2 (under higher trade volume) when facing higher free trade price relative to the reference price. The results show that the Nash equilibrium trade policy does not necessarily lead to further increases in the international market price when the government's balancing preference is for price stability and storage revenue. According to these predictions, storage policy has a price stabilization effect on the international market price.

5.3.2 *China's role in the world cotton market*

China plays a critical role in the international cotton market, involving sizable consumption, being the world's largest importer and the

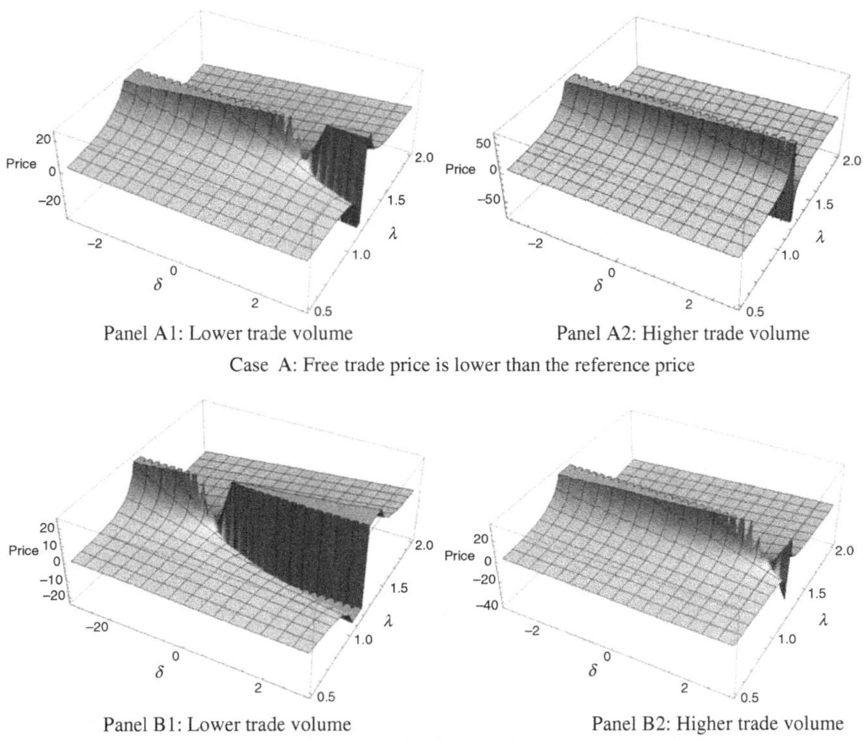

Fig. 5.2   Nash world price as functions of preference for price stability and storage revenue.

second-largest producer (Table 5.1) in 2014. China's cotton production accounted for around a quarter of the world's production and had been ranking number one before 2014, in which year it was exceeded by India. China consumes more than 30% of the world's cotton production. That means it still imports a large amount of cotton from the world market, and relatively little cotton produced in China is exported to other countries.

Between 2011 and 2014, China amassed 65,632 million 480lb bales of cotton, which is equivalent to more than 55% of the total world's production in 2014. This abnormal behavior of China has meant that it doubled the world cotton stock compared to average levels since 1950 (MacDonald *et al.*, 2015). China has become the

Table 5.1   China's role in the international cotton market.

Year	Production (Million 480lb bales)	Share of world production (%)	World Rank No.	Consumption (Million 480lb bales)	Share of world consumption (%)	World Rank No.
2000	20.30	22.78	1	23.50	25.49	1
2005	28.40	24.41	1	45.00	38.45	1
2010	30.50	25.94	1	46.00	39.73	1
2014	30.00	25.13	2	35.50	31.91	1
2000	0.23	0.88	25	26.16	1.69	13
2005	19.28	43.17	1	44.71	0.08	N/A
2010	11.98	32.58	1	35.36	0.34	26
2014	7.30	21.35	1	34.24	0.15	N/A

Notes: (1) Data are from NCCA; (2) N/A means that China does not rank in top 30.

main source of world cotton market uncertainty due to its trade volatility and its unpredictable storage policy.

The unprecedented domestic cotton policies and the critical role of China in the world market have attracted much attention from other main cotton producers (United States, India, Pakistan, Brazil, and Australia) and some international organizations (WTO, OECD, and NCCA). Numerous small cotton-exporting countries also care about the cotton policy in China, notably Benin, Burkina Faso, Chad, Mali, and Uzbekistan.

5.4 Data and Methodology

5.4.1 *Data and variables*

The dataset consists of annual observations between 1970 and 2014, including prices, world production, consumption, China storage, and the storage of the ROW. The "A" index is a proxy for the world price of cotton. It is an average of the cheapest five quotations from a selection of the principal upland kinds of cotton traded internationally.[6]

---

[6] See *https://www.cotlook.com/information/the-cotlook-a-index-plus-an-explanation/*.

Table 5.2 Overview of data and sources.

Variable name	Coverage	Units	Description	Source
CROPA	1975–2014	cents/pound	World cotton price	NCCA (2015)
PRODUCTION	1975–2014	(000) 480-pound bales	World cotton production	NCCA (2015)
CONSUMPTION	1975–2014	(000) 480-pound bales	World cotton consumption	NCCA (2015)
CESTOCK	1975–2014	(000) 480-pound bales	China cotton ending stocks	NCCA (2015)
ESEXCLUDCHINA	1975–2014	(000) 480-pound bales	World cotton ending stocks excluding China	NCCA (2015)

Table 5.3 Basic statistics of variables.

Variables	No. Observ.	Mean	Std. Dev	Min	Max
LN(CROPA)	40	4.27	0.24	3.73	5.11
LN(PRODUCTION)	40	11.38	0.24	10.90	11.76
LN(CONSUMPTION)	40	11.37	0.21	11.01	11.73
LN(CESTOCK)	40	10.62	0.44	9.93	11.61
LN(ESEXCLUDCHINA)	40	10.22	0.29	9.71	10.70

Notes: All the variables are expressed in logarithms.

The time series data, covering 40 years, range from 1975 to 2014 (Table 5.2). All the variables' data are collected from the NCCA website.[7] The units for world cotton prices and other variables, including production, consumption, and stocks, are in cents/pound and (000) 480-pound bales, respectively. We decompose the total world cotton storage into China's cotton storage and the cotton storage of the ROW. Table 5.3 reports the summary statistics of the variables. The standard deviation of China's storage is almost twice that of the world

---

[7] See *http://www.cotton.org/*.

price, production, consumption, and the world storage excluding China. China's unanticipated changes of cotton storage exaggerate the uncertainty in the world cotton market. The world cotton price, production, consumption, and world cotton storage excluding China approximately have the same variations except that the storage of the ROW has slightly higher fluctuations.

5.4.2 *Setting the VAR model*

The general VAR model in matrix form is simply

$$\Upsilon_t = \mu + \sum_{i=1}^{j} \beta_i \Upsilon_{t-1} + \varepsilon_t \tag{23}$$

Υ refers to all the endogenous variables, μ is a vector containing deterministic terms, and β is the coefficient matrix. If the equation form is expanded, we get the following equations:

$$
\begin{cases}
p_t = \mu_p^0 + \mu_p^t t + \sum_{i=1}^{j} \beta_i^p p_{t-i} + \sum_{i=1}^{j} \beta_i^q q_{t-i} + \sum_{i=1}^{j} \beta_i^x x_{t-i} + \sum_{i=1}^{j} \beta_i^z z_{t-i} \\
\quad + \sum_{i=1}^{j} \beta_i^s s_{t-i} + \varepsilon_t^p \\
q_t = \mu_q^0 + \mu_q^t t + \sum_{i=1}^{j} \beta_i^p p_{t-i} + \sum_{i=1}^{j} \beta_i^q q_{t-i} + \sum_{i=1}^{j} \beta_i^x x_{t-i} + \sum_{i=1}^{j} \beta_i^z z_{t-i} \\
\quad + \sum_{i=1}^{j} \beta_i^s s_{t-i} + \varepsilon_t^q \\
x_t = \mu_x^0 + \mu_x^t t + \sum_{i=1}^{j} \beta_i^p p_{t-i} + \sum_{i=1}^{j} \beta_i^q q_{t-i} + \sum_{i=1}^{j} \beta_i^x x_{t-i} + \sum_{i=1}^{j} \beta_i^z z_{t-i} \\
\quad + \sum_{i=1}^{j} \beta_i^s s_{t-i} + \varepsilon_t^x \\
s_t = \mu_s^0 + \mu_s^t t + \sum_{i=1}^{j} \beta_i^p p_{t-i} + \sum_{i=1}^{j} \beta_i^q q_{t-i} + \sum_{i=1}^{j} \beta_i^x x_{t-i} + \sum_{i=1}^{j} \beta_i^z z_{t-i} \\
\quad + \sum_{i=1}^{j} \beta_i^s s_{t-i} + \varepsilon_t^z \\
z_t = \mu_z^0 + \mu_z^t t + \sum_{i=1}^{j} \beta_i^p p_{t-i} + \sum_{i=1}^{j} \beta_i^q q_{t-i} + \sum_{i=1}^{j} \beta_i^x x_{t-i} + \sum_{i=1}^{j} \beta_i^z z_{t-i} \\
\quad + \sum_{i=1}^{j} \beta_i^s s_{t-i} + \varepsilon_t^z
\end{cases}
$$

$$\tag{24}$$

μ^0 is the constant term and μ^t is the time trend. We treat all the variables as endogenous variables for this first step in which we test the explanatory ability and function of the VAR model. In addition, we assume all cotton is homogenous across countries, and there is no trade distortion in the VAR system.

The variables are defined as follows:

- p_t: nominal world price (LN(CROPA)), crop year consistent with the crop year production, consumption, and storage variables;
- q_t: total world cotton production (LN(PRODUCTION));
- x_t: total world consumption in period t (LN(CONSUMPTION));
- z_t: world cotton stocks in period t and China is excluded (LN(ESEXCLUDCHINA));
- s_t: cotton storage in China in period t (LN(CESTOCK));
- $z_t + s_t$: total world cotton storage.

5.5 Diagnostic Tests, Estimation, and Forecast Evaluations

5.5.1 *Stationary tests*

More than 90% of agricultural tiDme series data are not stationary. Table 5.4 reports the basic diagnostic tests for the data stationary characteristic. In the process of testing, the ADF test (Dickey and Fuller, 1979) and the KPSS test (Kwiathowski *et al.*, 1992) are applied. Columns 1 and 3 report that most of the variables are not stationary, including the world cotton price, total production and consumption, China's cotton storage, and the storage of the ROW. If the first difference is taken for each variable, all the time series are stationary with 5% significance level at least, regardless of whether we include a constant term, trend, or lag numbers.

5.5.2 *Fix the lags of the dependent variables*

Three lag lengths are chosen based on the criteria reported in Table 5.5, bearing in mind that the maximum lag is four due to the limited sample size. Based on the criteria of FPE, AIC, HQIC, and SBIC, we finally fix the lag number at three for VAR estimation. The test results indicate that we have 36 observations and the sample is from 1979 to 2014.

Table 5.4 Unit root tests on data series during 1975–2014.

Variables	ADF (levels)*	ADF (1st diff.)	KPSS (level)	KPSS (1st diff.)
LN (CROPA)	−0.1275** (C, 0, 0)	−7.1191*** (C, 0, 0)	−3.4557** (C, 0, 0)	−7.1191*** (C, 0, 0)
	−3.4067 (C, T, 0)	−7.0244*** (C, T, 0)	−3.4067 (C, T, 0)	−7.0244*** (C, T, 0)
	−0.1275 (0, 0, 0)	−7.2237*** (0, 0, 0)	−0.1013 (0, 0, 0)	−7.2237*** (0, 0, 0)
LN (PRODUCTION)	−1.8187 (C, 0, 0)	−7.4613*** (C, 0, 0)	−1.7560 (C, 0, 0)	−7.5788*** (C, 0, 0)
	−4.5165*** (C, T, 0)	−7.4142*** (C, T, 0)	−4.5165*** (C, T, 0)	−7.5292*** (C, T, 0)
	−1.2881 (0, 0, 0)	−7.1803*** (0, 0, 0)	2.0871 (0, 0, 0)	−7.2361*** (0, 0, 0)
LN (CONSUMPTION)	−1.1602 (C, 0, 0)	−5.8447*** (C, 0, 0)	−1.1602 (C, 0, 0)	−5.8447*** (C, 0, 0)
	−1.8322 (C, T, 0)	−5.8835*** (C, T, 0)	−1.9778 (C, T, 0)	−5.8835*** (C, T, 0)
	2.0974 (0, 0, 0)	−5.2773*** (0, 0, 0)	2.0974 (0, 0, 0)	−5.2773*** (0, 0, 0)
LN (CESTOCK)	−0.7762 (C, 0, 0)	−4.2562*** (C, 0, 0)	−1.0189 (C, 0, 0)	−4.3500*** (C, 0, 0)
	−2.5578 (C, T, 0)	−4.1914** (C, T, 0)	−2.9073 (C, T, 0)	−4.2944*** (C, T, 0)
	−0.8872 (0, 0, 0)	−4.1966*** (0, 0, 0)	0.7831 (0, 0, 0)	−4.3024*** (0, 0, 0)
LN (ESEXCLUDCHINA)	−1.4326 (C, 0, 0)	−7.9096*** (C, 0, 0)	−0.8653 (C, 0, 0)	−8.0817*** (C, 0, 0)
	−3.9864** (C, T, 0)	−7.8048*** (C, T, 0)	−3.9864** (C, T, 0)	−7.9723*** (C, T, 0)
	0.7729 (0, 0, 0)	−7.8043*** (0, 0, 0)	1.6666 (0, 0, 0)	−7.9249*** (0, 0, 0)

Notes: (1) All the five variables are expressed in logarithms; (2) Testing format: C-constant; T-Trends; K-lag number; (3) Statistical significance is indicated with *(10%), **(5%), and ***(1%).

Table 5.5 Selection-order criteria output.

Lag No.	LL	LR	d.f	p	FPE	AIC	HQIC	SBIC
0	58.4606	—	—	—	5.7e–07	–3.02559	–2.96418	–2.84964
1	213.695	310.47	16	0.000	2.5e–10*	–10.7608	–10.4538*	–9.8811*
2	227.692	27.995	16	0.032	2.9e–10	–10.6496	–10.0969	–9.06606
3	245.975	36.566	16	0.002	2.8e–10	–10.7764*	–9.97808	–8.4891
4	261.766.	31.582*	16	0.011	2.4e–10	–10.7648	–9.72082	–7.7737

5.5.3 *Cointegration test and equations test*

After fixing the lag numbers and checking the units of the variables, it is time to test the long-run relationships between variables and the tolerance of the VRA model. According to the unrestricted cointegration rank test, we could have long-term equilibrium between variables. Table 5.6 presents the test, equation by equation. The R-squared values are high for each of the equations, indicating that the total explanation of each model is high. The residual normality is tested and reported in row five (Jarque-Bera), and we could not reject the null hypobook test that the residual is normally distributed.

Even on testing the stationarity of the five time series variables, we could visually follow that all the eigenvalues lie within the unit circle as shown in Fig. 5.3. Further tests confirm that the VAR model is stable.

5.5.4 *Model evaluation based on two types of forecasts*

The best application of the VAR model is forecast and a precise forecast offers the best criteria to judge the tolerability and function of the model. Figure 5.4 presents the within-sample prediction of world cotton price between 1975 and 2014. The reproduced historical data match the real-world cotton price quite well.

Given the within-sample forecast, we estimate the VAR model based on the subsample between 1975 and 2010. We forecast China's cotton storage, cotton storage of the ROW, and the world cotton

Table 5.6 Results of equation by equation diagnostic tests.

	LN (CESTOCK)	LN (CONSUMPTION)	LN (CROPA)	LN (ESEXCLUDCHINA)	LN (PRODUCTION)
S.E. equation	0.289615	0.038825	0.133962	0.119777	0.067227
R^2	0.943253	0.977335	0.853132	0.902336	0.736235
Adj. R^2	0.895282	0.958249	0.711032	0.820093	0.514116
Prob.(F)	19.70193	51.20594	6.382549	10.97156	3.314606
Jarque-Bera	0.9123	0.4229	0.3939	0.7259	0.4985

Notes: The individual coefficients are not reported here, which is not our interest.

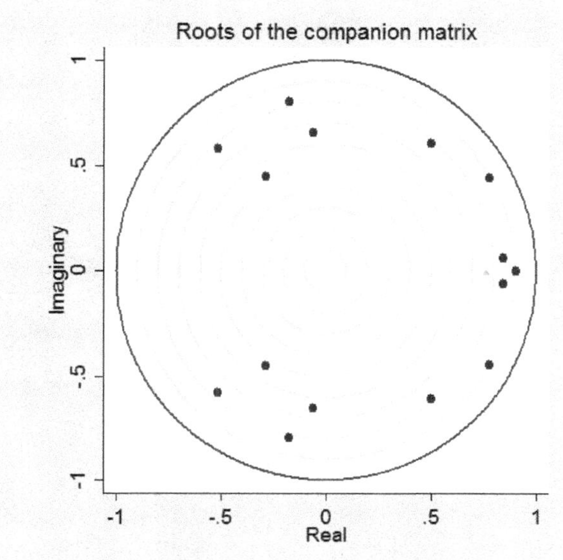

Fig. 5.3   VAR model's stability test.

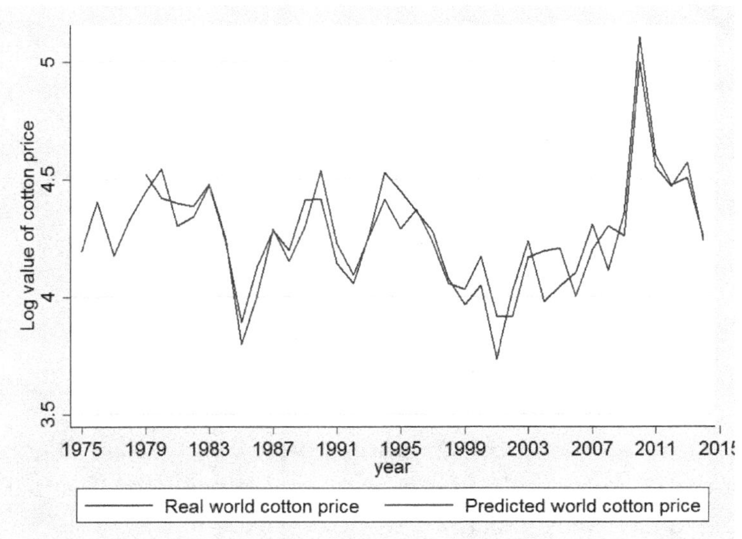

Fig. 5.4   Within-sample prediction of VAR model.

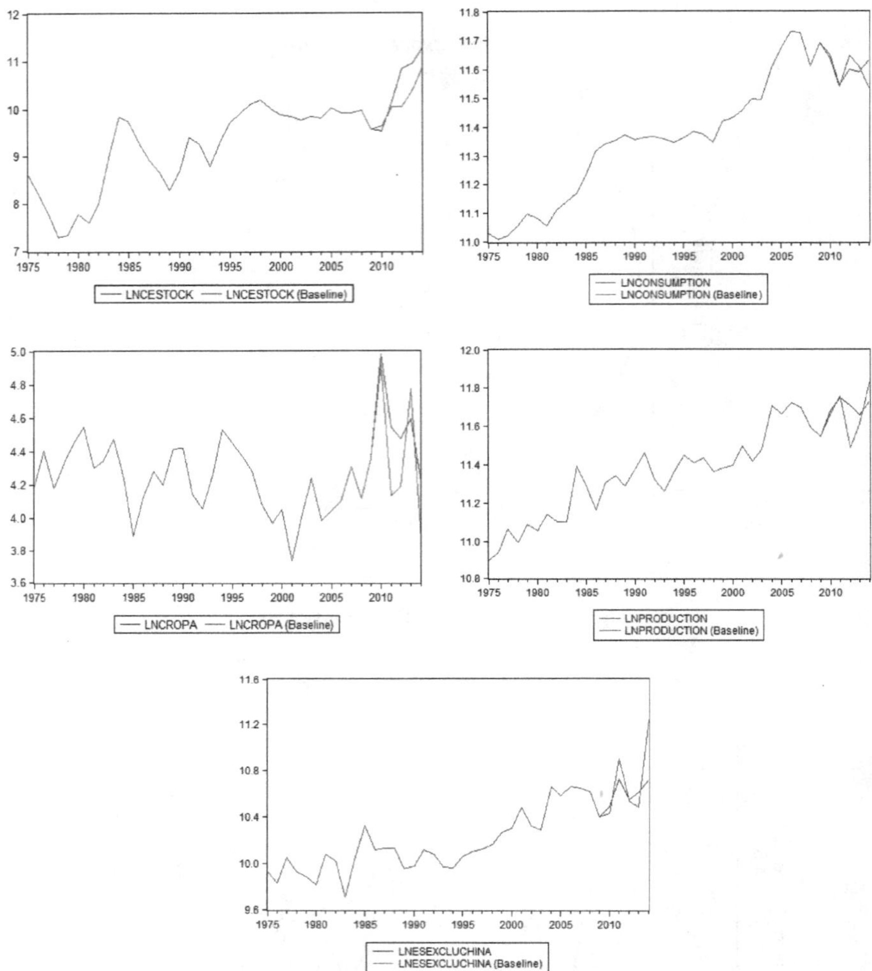

Fig. 5.5   Out-of-sample forecast between 2011 and 2014.

price, production, and consumption from 2011 to 2014. Figure 5.5 shows the out-of-sample forecast results compared with actual data. The out-of-sample predictions work as well. Jointly considering the within-sample prediction and out-of-sample test of the VAR model, the explanatory ability of our VAR model seems strong.

5.5.5 *Dynamic interactions between variables*

Now, the VAR model is adopted to identify the dynamic interactions between different variables using Impulse Response Functions (IRF) and Forecast Error Variance Decompositions (FEVD).

5.5.5.1 *Impulse response*

The impulse response function is used to get the response of one variable to unexpected changes in all other variables. Figure 5.6 represents the responses of world cotton price to the shocks of China's cotton storage, world consumption, the change of the world cotton price itself, cotton storage of the ROW, and total world production. The responses of the world cotton price to the unforeseen changes in China's cotton storage decrease for the first two periods and then rise from period three. China's cotton storage has a large effect on the world cotton market price in the first period. Comparing the responses to China's cotton storage with the responses to storage of the ROW, the effect in the first period is negative, but, from period two, the responses are persistently positive. The response of the world cotton price to China's cotton storage turns to positive one period later than responses to the storage of the ROW.

Regarding the responses of the international market cotton price to the shocks of consumption and production, total world consumption matters more than world production. As for consumption response, after a small level increase initially, it then sharply turns to a decrease for one period and then, in period three, it increases markedly. The dynamic responses to total world consumption are more complicated than we expected. In contrast to world consumption, world production takes fewer turns. The international cotton price responds to the production shocks four periods later. The world shock itself is positive for the first three periods with a continuously declining trend, and then it stabilizes with negative values.

To sum up, (1) the responses of world cotton market price to China's storage and the storage of the ROW are quite different,

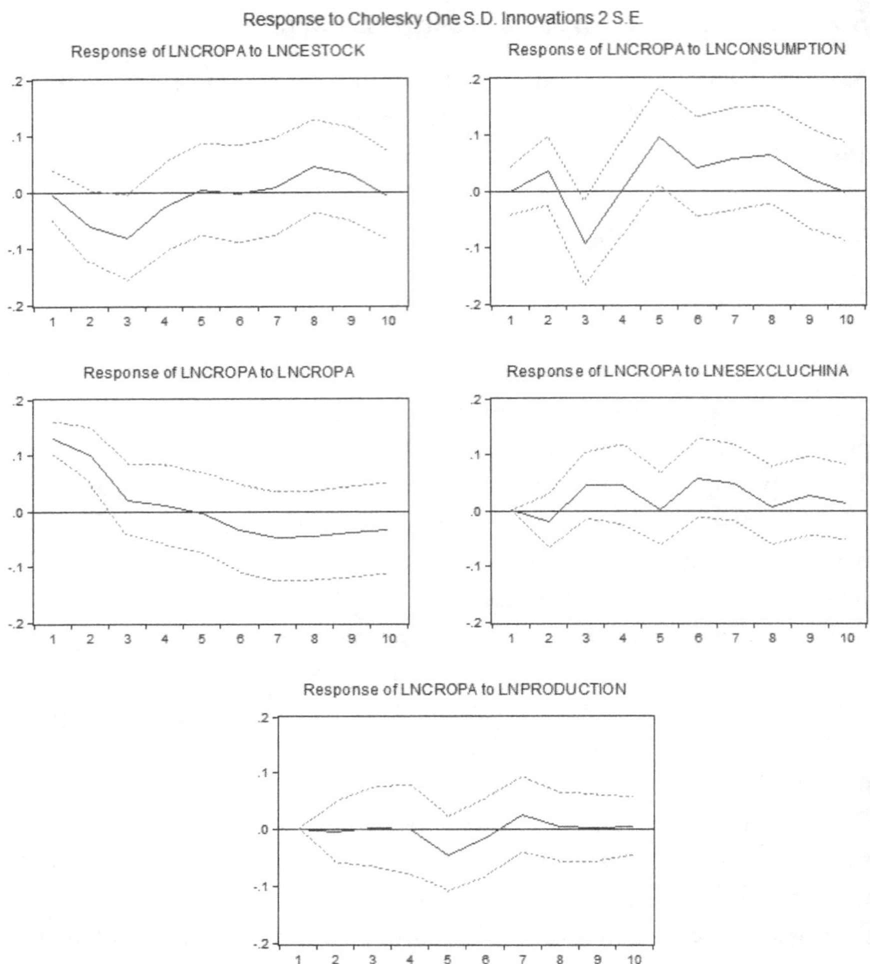

Fig. 5.6   Responses of world cotton price to changes in all other variables.

particularly in period two and period three; (2) consumption shocks matter more than production shocks; and (3) the complex dynamic relationships between world cotton price, China's cotton storage, cotton storage of the ROW, cotton consumption, and production suggest that a static partial equilibrium model would be inadequate.

5.5.5.2 *Forecast error variance decompositions*

Forecast error variance decomposition analysis answers the question as to how much of the forecast error variance in each of the variables can be explained by other variables. Figure 5.7 presents the contributions of each variable to forecast variance change within the horizon. As with the variance decomposition of China's cotton storage, the most important contributors are world cotton consumption and the world market cotton price. The role of the world cotton price is higher than that of consumption for the first four periods. World cotton production and the storage of the ROW play a limited role in influencing China's cotton storage, which is consistent with impulse response analysis. China's cotton storage takes the highest weight in the variance decomposition of total world consumption. The world price ranks number two followed by world production, which ranks number three, while the storage of the ROW has a minimal effect. In the short term, China's cotton storage ranks number one in world cotton price variance decomposition, rather than consumption, which takes the highest weight three periods later. In the variance decomposition of the storage of the ROW, world cotton consumption, China's cotton storage, world cotton price, and world production rank from number one to number four, respectively. China's cotton storage has the highest weight concerning world production variance decomposition, and the other three contributors' roles are parallel to the expansion in time.

In brief, the role of China's cotton storage has the highest weight in the variance decomposition in terms of world consumption, production, and the first three periods of world cotton price. This is consistent with our hypobook that China's cotton storage does affect world cotton production. The role of world consumption, which takes the most important weight just after two or three periods, is higher than production. The result is consistent with our expectation that international trade across countries could mitigate the effects of production shocks globally.

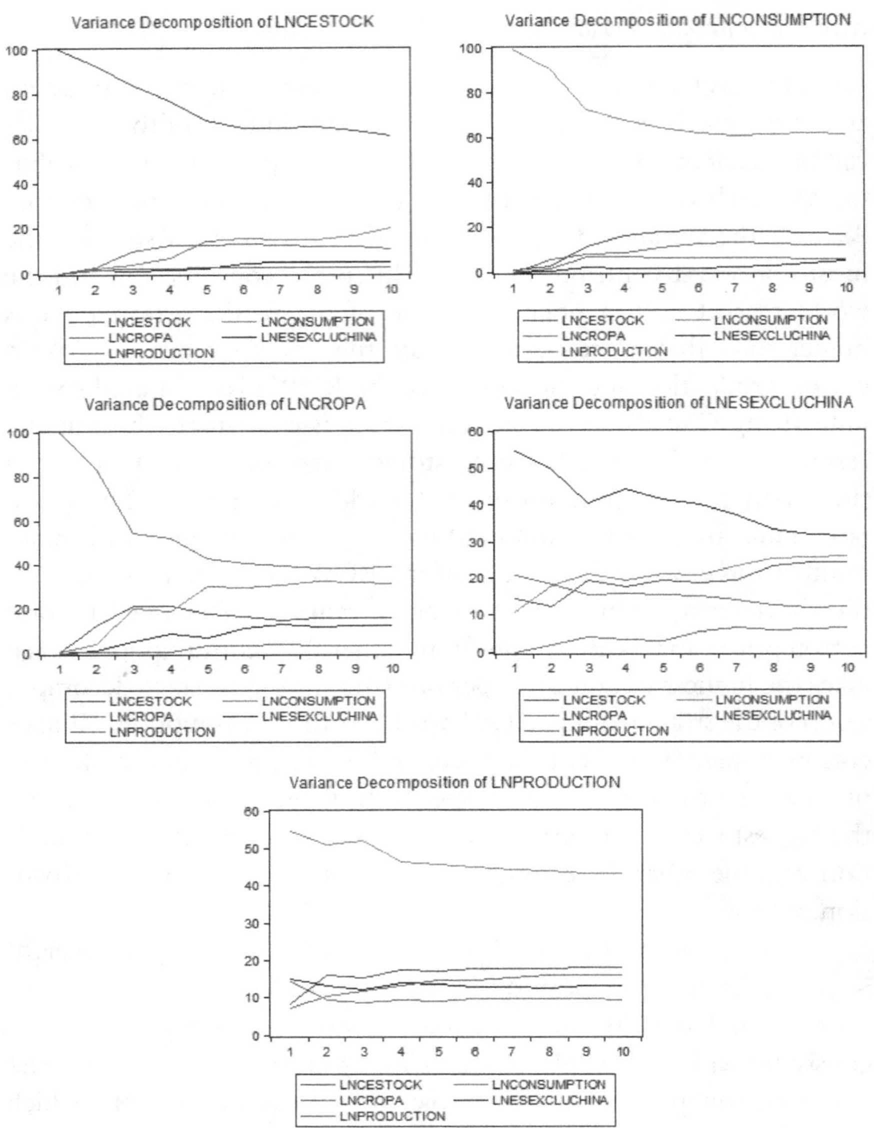

Fig. 5.7   Forecast error variance decomposition.

5.6 Simulations

5.6.1 *Does China's storage cause the world cotton price to change?*

Having investigated each variable's response to unforeseen shocks of other variables, we now explore the effects of China's cotton storage on the world cotton price, which will be tested by Granger causality.[8]

Table 5.7 reports the Granger causality test results. The last row indicates that past information could provide valuable data for current values for each of the five dependent variables (columns 1–5). Our most interesting variable is China's cotton storage. The columns in Table 5.7 show that world cotton consumption, production, world price, and the storage of the ROW are not the cause of China's cotton storage in that each test does not reject the null hypobook. Regarding the second-to-last row, China's cotton storage is not Granger causality for other variables in the VAR system.

The Granger causality test results suggest that past values of China's cotton storage do not help forecast current values of other variables. Conversely, the past information on world cotton consumption, production, world price, and the storage of the ROW is also not useful in making current China's cotton storage forecasts. China's cotton storage is quite possibly irrelevant for the VAR system, and we could treat China's cotton storage as an exogenous variable. This is consistent with previous research that suggests China's storage policy is aimed at the domestic self-sufficiency target and is irrelevant to the world market (Dawe *et al.*, 2009).

5.6.2 *Simulating the effects of a reduction of China's cotton storage*

Based on the tests above, China's cotton storage can be considered an exogenous variable in the VAR system. Myers *et al.* (1990) put

---

[8] Likelihood ratio test (Sims, 1980) is formally applied here.

Table 5.7 Results of block exogeneity (Granger causality) test.[a]

	Exclude LNCESTOCK	Exclude LNCONSUMPTION	Exclude LNCROPA	Exclude LNESEXCLUCHINA	Exclude LNPRODUCTION
LNCONSUMPTION	2.138208	—	22.28182***	3.608608	2.607298
LNCROPA	4.705642	12.02402***	—	1.069429	2.909880
LNESEXCLUCHINA	7.009195	1.599387	3.061816	—	2.775533
LNPRODUCTION	5.652870	1.953656	0.591033	2.234861	—
LNCESTOCK	—	0.145530	2.869948	5.664711	1.806506
All	22.78387***	22.82222***	66.79397***	18.11659	29.10377***

Notes: (1) The values in the table mean the chi-sq. value; (2) ***significantly different from zero at 1% significant level.
[a]In the model identification step, the lagged number is fixed at three.

forward the theory relating to counterfactual simulation. A percentage reduction of China's cotton storage from 2011 to 2014 is used in the dynamic stochastic simulation. This simulation is based on one assumption, which is that the VAR model still describes the data as accurately as the originally set model. The real data series are the benchmark line of the counterfactual scenario simulations. The exogenous condition is satisfied based on the Granger causality test above. We could decrease China's cotton storage by some percentage to create the counterfactual. The dynamic simulation is run with world cotton production, consumption, world cotton price, and the storage of the ROW.

In the following, we create two scenarios by decreasing China's cotton storage by 20% and 50% to see the responses of other variables, particularly the world cotton price. Figure 5.8 shows the counterfactual results of changing China's cotton storage. The decreasing of China's cotton storage (Panel A) results in a dramatic decline of the world cotton production. The storage of the ROW would decrease subsequently too. The most interesting outcome is that the world cotton price would be much higher than the realized price during 2011–2014. World cotton consumption would decrease a bit even if world consumption has less impact on the world price based on the impulse response test and forecast error variance decompositions.

Even China's cotton price increases the uncertainty of the international market. China's cotton storage during 2011–2014 does not drive up and contribute to the fluctuations of world cotton market prices. Based on the dynamic simulation results, we can conclude that China's cotton storage between 2011 and 2014 functioned as a signal which stimulated the total world production and drove the world price down from the peak level in 2010. Meanwhile, China's storage policy between 2011 and 2014 contributed to returning the world cotton price from the highest level of the past 50 years in 2010 to a more normal level.

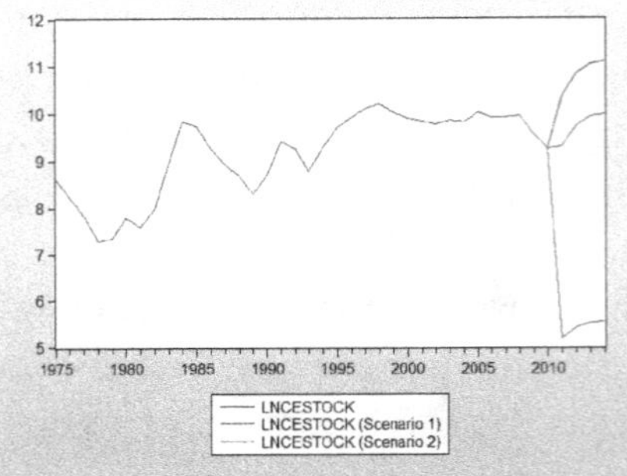

Panel A: Cotton storage change of China

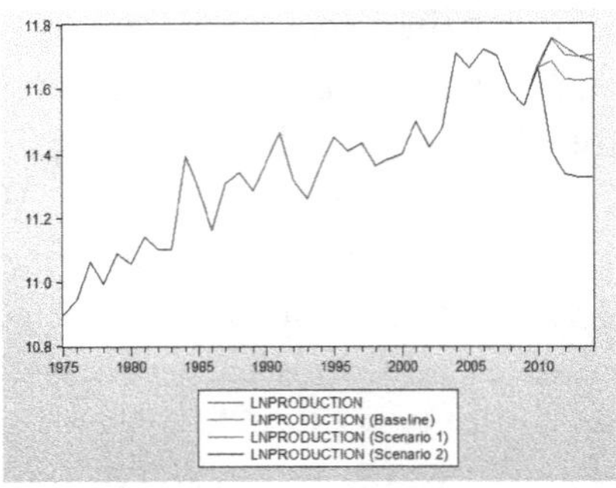

Panel B: Changes of world cotton production

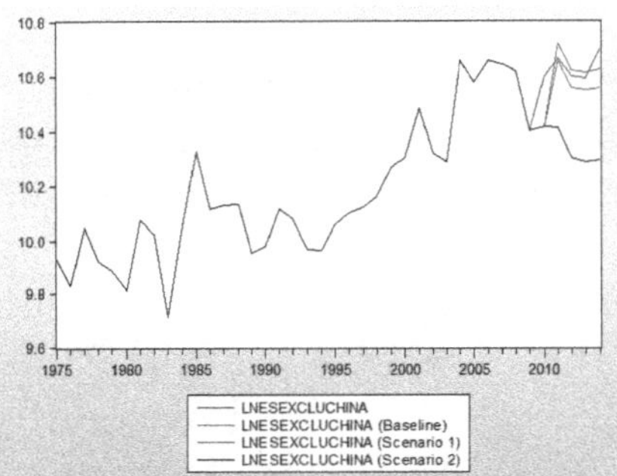

Panel C: Storage changes of the ROW

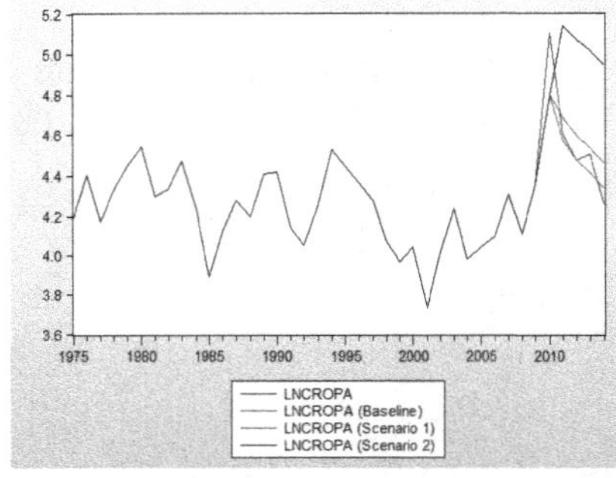

Panel D: Changes of world cotton price

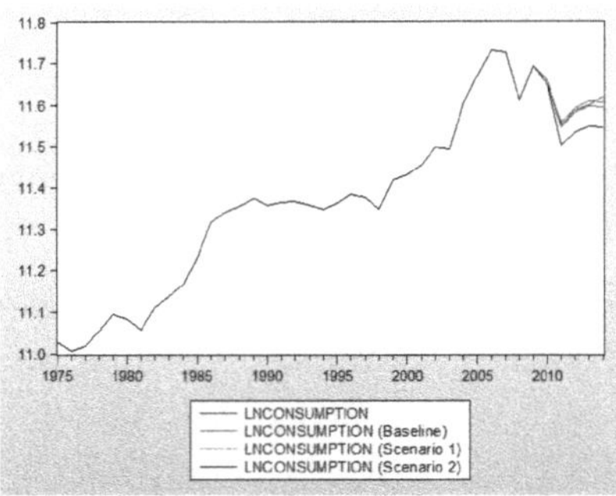

Panel E: Changes of world cotton consumption

Fig. 5.8   Simulations of decreasing China's cotton storage by 20% (Scenario 1) and 50% (Scenario 2).

5.7 Conclusions

This chapter first sets out a political economy model to explore the government's motivations for a national storage policy in the context of border and domestic policy coordination. The theoretical model predicts that domestic storage policy could not only strengthen price stabilization but also increase its social welfare. However, the effects of the two instruments on the Nash equilibrium international market price are in opposite directions. It implies that the world market price is not monotonically increasing with respect to trade policy interventions when domestic storage policy is incorporated in the theoretical model. This means that domestic storage policy has the potential to have a price stabilization effect in both the domestic and international market.

China dominates the world's storage of cotton and it provides ideal experimental data to identify the effects of China's cotton storage policy (in combinations with its cotton trade and subsidy policy) on the world cotton market. The VAR method used to model those effects shows that domestic public storage could indeed contribute to the stabilization of the international market price of cotton. These simulated dynamic relationships indicate that a counterfactual decline of China's cotton storage between 2011 and 2014 would depress world production and suppress storage in the ROW, which in turn would lead to an increase in the world cotton market price and a decline of world cotton consumption.

6

Conclusion and Policy Implications

6.1 Concluding Remarks

This book contributes to our understanding of the motivations and effects of agricultural price-distorting policies both theoretically and empirically in China, and from both long- and short-term perspectives. Only with such an understanding of the reasons behind choices is it possible to have an influence on policy reforms aimed at developing the economy and improving social welfare.

The Chinese government has transitioned from taxing heavily to persistently subsidizing the agricultural sector. Chapter 2 theoretically presents the simultaneous economic and political driving forces behind China's changing agricultural protection levels, by extending the specific factor model in a traditional dual economy to three sectors. The results indicate that switching from taxing to subsidizing the agricultural sector not only depends on changes in the economy's structure but more critically on the underlying political support from key interest groups in the course of economic development in China.

Chapter 3 focuses on the differences between China and the ROW in their driving forces affecting their agricultural policymaking during 1981–2010. Based on a two-way fixed-effects regression model, two main findings emerge. First, arable land per capita, the employment share in the agricultural sector, and the self-sufficiency ratio are more important explanators for China than for the ROW. Second, the Chinese government cares more about inequality than poverty when determining agricultural distortions.

Understanding how governments respond to short-term world price fluctuations is the focus of Chapter 4. It sets out a theoretical model based on a political economy framework that incorporates behavior economics. The trackable model is applied to China which is a one-party government dealing with geographically based minority interest groups. Politically sensitive products are formally defined, and the model assumes that individuals' preferences are characterized by loss aversion and reference dependence. The government not only cares about the aggregate social welfare but also about political support from politically sensitive groups that produce a politically sensitive product. The theoretical model predictions are that politically sensitive products receive higher protection from the government, and that the government alters trade restrictions to insulate the domestic market from international price spikes. Furthermore, our theory reveals that the international terms of trade play a critical role in determining trade policies.

China is a large agricultural producing and consuming country, particularly in cotton, and it has a large impact on the world cotton market. In order to uncover the effects of loss aversion from producers and consumers, which may be confounded by terms of trade effects, the theoretical model of Chapter 4 is extended to a large country. The model predictions of the small country model are still robust in the large country case. The model is empirically tested and found to explain China's cotton protection policy: When the world price is higher than the reference price, the government takes a lower protection level, and the government applies a higher protection level when world price is lower than the reference price. China does so by altering trade restrictions to insulate the domestic market from short-term fluctuations in the international price.

Chapters 2–4 improve our understanding of the underlying causes of distorted agricultural trade-related polices theoretically and empirically for China. However, variations in trade restrictions by many countries in response to international price spikes exacerbate those spikes. That encourages governments to also use domestic storage policies to cope with fluctuating international prices. China has stored large amounts of agricultural products during recent years, including rice, wheat, and maize, and also cotton. Chapter 5 theoretically explores the government's motivations for its storage policy in the context of policy coordination. The theoretical model predicts that the domestic storage policy could not only strengthen price stabilization but also reinforce the price-insulating trade policy and increase social welfare. However, the effects of the two instruments on the Nash equilibrium international market price are in opposite directions. It implies that the world market price is not monotonically increasing in terms of trade policy interventions when domestic storage policy is incorporated into the theoretical model. These results also indicate that the domestic storage policy can have a price stabilization effect not only on the domestic market but also on the international market price.

In terms of cotton, China is considered a leader in the world market and cotton storage has climbed to 66 billion 480lb bales, which equates to more than 55% of the world's total production in 2014. Identifying and simulating the effects of China's cotton storage policy on the world market is the other research focus of Chapter 5. Based on the cotton data from 1975 to 2014, a VAR model is used to identify the effects of China's cotton storage on the world cotton market. According to the block exogeneity test, China's cotton storage is an exogenous variable in the VAR system. The dynamic simulation results show that the sharp increase of China cotton storage contributed to the fall in the world cotton price from the record level in 2010 to a more normal price by 2014. That chapter concludes that China's domestic public storage has had a price-stabilizing effect[1] on the world market price.

---

[1] The price stabilization effect means China's cotton storage drives back the international price level toward its trend level, rather than changing the variance of the world market price.

6.2 Policy Implications

The findings of this book have strong policy implications. The first implication has to do with the Chinese government's ongoing efforts to solve the "three agriculture issues" of persistent poverty, increased inequality between farm and non-farm households, and food insecurity. The Chinese government should not apply trade distortions at the expense of resource allocation efficiency, social welfare, and higher consumption prices for consumers. More efficient ways to solve current social problems could be relaxing unskilled labor mobility by the *Hukou* System Reform and the Rural Land Circulation Reform, increasing education levels and technical skills of unskilled laborers with the help of training programs, enhancing agricultural productivity by investing in research and technological innovation, and decreasing trade costs by infrastructure investment and information communication improvement.

As for short-term agricultural price fluctuations, the government's use of trade restrictions to stabilize the domestic market by insulating it from international price spikes is having distortionary effects that are adding to price and trade volume fluctuation on world markets. An optimally managed domestic storage policy could have the opposite effect on the international market price to trade policy. However, if it is badly managed, such storage policies could further exacerbate instability in international markets. The Chinese government could instead apply more generic forms of assistance to farm households in areas left behind such as Xinjiang.

Bibliography

Abbott, P. C. (2011). Export restrictions as stabilization responses to food crisis. *American Journal of Agricultural Economics* **94**(2), 428–434.

Acemoglu, D. and Robinson, J. A. (2006). *Economic Origins of Dictatorship and Democracy*. New York: Cambridge University Press.

Acemoglu, D. and Robinson, J. A. (2012). *Why Nations Fail: The Origins of Power, Prosperity, and Poverty*. New York: Crown Publishers.

Anderson, K. (1992). International dimensions of political economy of distortionary price and trade policies. In I. Goldin and L. A. Winters (Eds.), *Open Economies: Structural Adjustment and Agriculture*. Cambridge and New York: Cambridge University Press.

Anderson, K. (1995a). Lobbying incentives and the pattern of protection in rich and poor countries. *Economic Development and Cultural Change* **43**(2), 401–423.

Anderson, K. (1995b). The political economy of coal subsidies in Europe. *Energy Policy* **23**(6), 485–496.

Anderson, K. (2009). *Distortions to Agricultural Incentives: A Global Perspective, 1955–2007*. London: Palgrave Macmillan and Washington DC: The World Bank.

Anderson, K. (2010). *The Political Economy of Agricultural Price Distortions*. Cambridge and New York: Cambridge University Press.

Anderson, K. (2012). Government trade restrictions and international price volatility. *Global Food Security* **1**(2), 157–166.

Anderson, K. (2013). Agricultural price distortions: Trends and volatility, past, and prospective. *Agricultural Economics* **44**(s1), 163–171.

Anderson, K., Cockburn, J. and Martin, W. (2010). *Agricultural Price Distortions, Inequality, and Poverty*. Washington DC: The World Bank.

Anderson, K. and Hayami, Y. (1986). *The Political Economy of Agricultural Protection: East Asia in International Perspective*. Bonson, London and Sydney: Allen and Unwin.

Anderson, K., Ivanic, M. and Martin, W. J. (2014). Food price spikes, price insulation, and poverty. In J.-P. Chavas, D. Hummels, and B. D. Weight (Eds.), *The Economics of Food Price Volatility* (pp. 311–344). Chicago and London: University of Chicago for NBER.

Anderson, K., Kurzweil, M., Martin, W., Sandri, D. and Valenzuela, E. (2008). Measuring distortions to agricultural incentives, revisited. *World Trade Review* 7(4), 675–704.

Anderson, K. and Nelgen, S. (2012a). Trade barrier volatility and agricultural price stabilization. *World Development* **40**(1), 36–48.

Anderson, K. and Nelgen, S. (2012b). Agricultural trade distortions during the global financial crisis. *Oxford Review of Economic Policy* **28**(2), 235–260.

Anderson, K. and Nelgen, S. (2012c). *Trade Policy for Loss Aversion: Evidence from Agriculture*. Paper presented at the 55th Annual Conference of the Australian Agricultural and Resource.

Anderson, K. and Nelgen, S. (2013). *Updated National and Global Estimates of Distortions to Agricultural Incentives, 1955 to 2011*. Retrieved from www. worldbank.org/agdistortions.

Anderson, K., Rausser, G. and Swinnen, J. (2013). Political economy of public policies: Insights from distortions to agricultural and food markets. *Journal of Economic Literature* **51**(2), 423–477.

Anderson, K. and Strutt, A. (2014). Food security policy options for China: Lessons from other countries. *Food Policy* **49**, 50–58.

Anderson, K. and Thennakoon, J. (2015). Food price spikes and poor, small economies: What role for trade policies. *African Journal of Agricultural and Resource Economics* **10**(1), 16–31.

Anderson, K. and Valenzuela, E. (2008). *Estimates of Global Distortions to Agricultural Incentives, 1955–2007*. Retrieved from: www.worldbank. org/agdistortions.

Arezki, R. and Brückner, M. (2011). *Food Prices and Political Instability*. IMF Working Paper: WP/11/62.

Baldwin, R.E. (1987). Political realistic objective functions and trade policy PROFs and tariff. *Economic Letters* **24**, 287–290.

Balisacan, A. M. and Roumasset, J. A. (1987). Public choice of economic policy: The growth of agricultural protection. *Weltwirtschaftliches Archiv Bd* (CXXII), 232–248.

Bates, R. H. and Block, S. (2010). Political economy of agricultural trade interventions in Africa. In K. Anderson (Ed.), *The Political Economy of Agricultural Price Distortions*. Cambridge and New York: Cambridge University Press.

Becker, G. S. (1983). A theory of competition among pressure groups for political influence. *The Quarterly Journal of Economics* **98**(3), 371–400.

Becker, G. S. (1985). Public policies, pressure groups, and dead weight costs. *Journal of Public Economics* **28**(3), 329–347.

Beghin, J. C. and Kherallah, M. (1994). Political institutions and international patterns of agricultural protection. *The Review of Economics and Statistics* **76**(3), 482–489.

Bellemare, M. F. (2014). Rising food prices, food price volatility, and social unrest. *American Journal of Agricultural Economics* **97**(1), 1–21.

Besley, T. and Persson, T. (2011). *Pillars of Prosperity: The Political Economics of Development Clusters*. United Kingdom: Princeton University Press.

Bhagwati, J. N. (1971). The generous theory of distortions and welfare. In J. N. Bhagwati, R. W. Jones, R. A. Mundell and J. Vanek (Eds.), *Trade, Balance of Payments and Growth*. Amsterdam: North-Holland.

Blanchard, E. and Willmann, G. (2013). *Unequal Gains, Prolonged Pain: Dynamic Adjustment Costs and Protectionist Overshooting*. NBER ITI Meeting.

Board of Governors of the Federal Reserve System. Foreign exchange rate-H.10: Historical data through 1989. Retrieved from: http://www.federalreserve. gov/releases/h10/hist/default1989.htm.

Bouët, A. and Laborde Debucquet, D. (2012). Food crisis and export taxation: The cost of non-cooperative trade policies. *Review of World Economics* **148**(1), 209–233.

Branstettera, L. G. and Feenstra, R. C. (2002). Trade and foreign direct investment in China: A political economy approach. *Journal of International Economics* **58**(2), 335–358.

Broda, C., Limão, N. and Weinstein, D. E. (2008). Optimal tariffs and market power: The evidence. *The American Economic Review* **98**(5), 2032–2065.

Bullock, D. S. (1994). In search of rational government: What political preference function studies measure and assume. *American Journal of Agricultural Economics* **76**(3), 347–361.

Chase, K. A. (2015). Domestic geography and policy pressures. In L. L. Martin (Ed.), *The Oxford Handbook of the Political Economy of International Trade*. Oxford, United Kingdom: Oxford University Press.

Chaudhuri, S. and Banerjee, D. (2010). Foreign capital inflow, skilled–unskilled wage inequality and unemployment of unskilled labor in a fair wage model. *Economic Modelling* **27**(1), 477–486.

China National Cotton Information Center. China cotton price. (2015). Retrieved from: http://www.cncotton.com/.

Corden, W. M. (1971). *The Theory of Protection*. Oxford: Clarendon Press.

Corden, W. M. (1997). *Trade Policy and Economic Welfare* (2nd Ed.): Clarendon Press.

David, C. C. and Huang, J. (1996). Political economy of rice price protection in Asia. *Economic Development and Cultural Change* **44**(3), 463–483.

Dawe, D., Morales-Opazo, C., Balie, J. and Pierre, G. (2015). How much have domestic food prices increased in the new era of higher food prices? *Global Food Security* **5**, 1–10.

de Gorter, H. and Tsur, Y. (1991). Explaining price policy bias in agriculture: The calculus of support-maximizing politicians. *American Journal of Agricultural Economics* **73**(4), 1244–1254.

Demeke, M. Pangrazio, G. and Maetz, M. (2009). Country responses to the food security crisis: Nature and preliminary implications of the policies pursued *Initiative on Soaring Food Prices*. Agricultural Policy Support Service, FAO, working paper U.S.

Dickey, D. A. and Fuller, W. A. (1979). Distribution of the estimators for autoregressive time series with a unit root. *Journal of the American Statistical Association* **74**(366), 427–431.

Dissanayake, J. (2014). *Political Economy of Altering Trade Restrictions*. SSNR Working Paper: No. 2539324.

Dominique Patton, R. (2015). China's top cotton producer is resisting the government's reforms. Retrieved from: http://www.businessinsider.com/r-top-china-cotton-producer-resists-reforms-in-restive-xinjiang-2015-2/?r=AU&IR=T.

Dutt, P. and Mitra, D. (2010). Impacts of ideology, inequality, lobbying, and public finance. In K. Anderson (Ed.), *The Political Economy of Agricultural Price Distortions*. Cambridge and New York: Cambridge University Press.

Feenstra, R. C. (2016). *Advanced International Trade: Theory and Evidence* (2nd Ed.). Princeton NJ: Princeton University Press.

Findlay, R. and Wellisz, S. (1982). Endogenous tariffs, the political economy of trade restrictions, and welfare. In J. N. Bhagwati (Ed.), *Import Competition and Response* (pp. 223–234). Chicago: University of Chicago Press.

Freund, C. and Özden, Ç. (2008). Trade policy and loss aversion. *American Economic Review* **98**(4), 1675–1691.

Fulginiti, L. E. and Shogren, J. F. (1992). Agricultural protection in developing countries. *American Journal of Agricultural Economics* **74**, 759–801.

Fulton, M. E. and Reynolds, T. (2015). The political economy of food price volatility: The case of Vietnam and rice. *American Journal of Agricultural Economics* **97**(4), 1206–1226.

Gardner, B. L. (1987). Causes of U.S. farm commodity programs. *Journal of Political Economy* **95**(2), 290–310.

Gawande, K. and Hoekman, B. (2006). Lobbying and agricultural trade policy in the United States. *International Organization* **60**(3), 527–561.

Gawande, K. and Hoekman, B. (2010). Why governments tax or subsidize trade: Evidence from agriculture. In K. Anderson (Ed.), *The Political Economy of Agricultural Price Distortions*. Cambridge and New York: Cambridge University Press.

Giordani, P. E., Rocha, N. and Ruta, M. (2016). Food prices and the multiplier effect of trade policy. *Journal of International Economics* **101**, 102–122.

Gollin, D. (2014). The Lewis Model: A 60-year retrospective. *Journal of Economic Perspectives* **28**(3), 71–88.

Gouel, C. (2012). Agricultural price instability: A survey of competing explanations and remedies. *Journal of Economic Surveys* **26**(1), 129–156.

Gouel, C. (2013). Optimal food price stabilization policy. *European Economic Review* **57**, 118–134.

Gouel, C. (2016). Trade policy coordination and food price volatility. *American Journal of Agricultural Economics* **98**(4), 1018–1037.

Gouel, C. and Jean, S. (2015). Optimal food price stabilization in a small open developing country. *The World Bank Economic Review* **29**(1), 72–101.

Grossman, G. M. and Helpman, E. (1994). Protection for sale. *The American Economic Review* **84**(4), 833–850.

Grossman, G. M. and Helpman, E. (1995). Trade war and trade talks. *Journal of Political Economy* **103**(4), 675–708.

Guo, R. (2015). *China's Spatial (Dis)integration: Political Economy of the Inter-ethnic Unrest in Xinjiang.* United Kingdom: Elsevier.

Harberger, A. C. (1971). Three basic postulates for applied welfare economics. *Journal of Economic Literature* **9**(3), 785–797.

Harris, J. R. and Todaro, M. P. (1970). Migration, unemployment and development: A two-sector analysis. *The American Economic Review* **20**(1), 126–142.

Hillman, A. L. (1982). Declining industries and political-support protectionist motives. *The American Economic Review* **72**(5), 1180–1187.

Honma, M. and Hayami, Y. (1987). Agricultural protection of East Asia in international perspective. *Asian Economic Journal* **1**(1), 48–69.

Huang, J., Yang, J. and Rozelle, S. (2015). The political economy of food price policy in China. In P. Pinstrup-Andersen (Ed.), *Food Price Policy in an Era of Market Instability: A Political Economy Analysis.* Oxford: Oxford University Press.

Ivanic, M. and Martin, W. (2014). Implications of domestic price insulation for global food price behavior. *Journal of International Money and Finance* **42**, 272–288.

Jean, S., Laborde, D. and Martin, W. (2011). Formulas and flexibility in trade negotiations: Sensitive agricultural products in the World Trade Organization's Doha Agenda. *World Bank Economic Review* **24**(3), 500–519.

Jones, R. W. (1971). A three-factor model in theory, trade, and history. In J. N. Bhagwati, R. W. Jones, R. A. Mundell and J. Vanek (Eds.), *Trade, Balance of Payments and Growth: Papers in International Economics in Honor of Charles P. Kindleberger* (pp. 3–21). Amsterdam. London: North-Holland Publishing Company.

Kaufmann, D. (2013). *Worldwide Governance Indicators.* Retrieved from: http://info.worldbank.org/governance/wgi/index.aspx#doc.

Krueger, A. O. (1992). *The Political Economy of Agricultural Pricing Policy: A Synbook of the Political Economy in Developing Countries.* Baltimore, MD: Johns Hopkins University Press.

Kwiatkowski, D., Phillips, P. C. B., Schmidt, P. and Shin, Y. (1992). Testing the null hypobook of stationarity against the alternative of a unit root. *Journal of Econometrics* **54**, 159–178.

Lewis, W. A. (1954). Economic development with unlimited supplies of labor. *The Manchester School* **22**(2), 139–191.

Li, K. (1991). Study on the tripartite structure of the economy in China. (In Chinese). *China Social Science* **3**, 65–82.

Lü, X., Scheve, K. and Slaughter, M. J. (2012). Inequity aversion and the international distribution of trade protection. *American Journal of Political Science* **56**(3), 638–654.

Ma, W. and Abdulai, A. (2016). Does cooperative membership improve household welfare? Evidence from apple farmers in China. *Food Policy* **58**, 94–102.

MacDonald, S., Gale, F. and Hansen, J. (2015). Cotton policy in China. United States: Economic Research Service, United States Department of Agriculture.

Magee, S. P., Brock, W. A. and Young, L. (1989). *Black Hole Tariffs and Endogenous Policy Theory: Political Economy in General Equilibrium.* Cambridge: Cambridge University Press.

Martin, W. (2009). Some support policy options for cotton in China. *China Agricultural Economic Review* **1**(1), 23–37.

Martin, W. and Anderson, K. (2011). Export restrictions and price insulation during commodity price booms. *American Journal of Agricultural Economics* **94**(2), 422–427.

Martin, W. and Anderson, K. (2012). Trade distortions and food price surges. In R. Arezki, C. A. Pattillo, M. Quintyn and M. Zhu (Eds.), *Commodity Price Volatility and Inclusive Growth in Low-Income Countries.* Washington, DC: International Monetary Fund.

Mayer, W. (1974). Short-run and long-run equilibrium for a small open economy. *Journal of Political Economy* **82**(5), 955–967.

Mayer, W. (1984). Endogenous tariff formation. *The American Economic Review* **74**(5), 970–985.

Melgar, N., Milgram-Baleix, J. and Rossi, M. (2013). Explaining protectionism support: The role of economic factors. *ISRN Economics* **2013**, 1–14.

Milanovic, B. (2005). *Worlds Apart: Measuring International and Global Inequality.* New Jersey United States: Princeton University Press.

Mussa, M. (1974). Tariffs and the distribution of income: The importance of factor specificity, substitutability, and intensity in the short and long run. *Journal of Political Economy* **82**(6), 1191–1203.

Myers, R. J., Piggott, R. R. and Tomek, W. G. (1990). Estimating sources of fluctuations in the Australian wool market: An application of VAR methods. *Australian Journal of Agricultural Economics* **34**(3), 242–262.

North, D. C., Wallis, J. J. and Weingast, B. R. (2009). *Violence and Social Orders: A Conceptual Framework for Interpreting Recorded Human History.* United States: Cambridge University Press.

Olper, A. (2001). Determinants of agricultural protection: The role of democracy and institutional setting. *Journal of Agricultural Economics* **52**(2), 75–92.

Olper, A. (2007). Land inequality, government ideology, and agricultural protection. *Food Policy* **32**(1), 67–83.

Olper, A., Fałkowski, J. and Swinnen, J. (2013). Political reforms and public policy: Evidence from agricultural and food policies. *The World Bank Economic Review* **28**(1), 21–47.

Olson, M. (1965). *The Logic of Collective Action*. Cambridge MA: Harvard University Press.

Persson, T. and Tabellini, G. (2000). *Political Economics Explaining Economic Policy*. Cambridge MA: MIT Press.

Pokrivcak, J., Swinnen, J. and Crombez, C. (2006). The *Status Quo* Bias and reform of the Common Agricultural Policy: Impact of voting rules, the European Commission and external changes. *European Review of Agricultural Economics* **33**(4), 562–590.

Rausser, G. C. (1982). *Political Economic Markets: PERTS and PESTS in Food and Agriculture*. CUDARE Working Papers: No. 231.

Rausser, G. C. and Freebairn, J. W. (1974). Estimation of policy preference functions: An application to U.S. beef import quota. *The Review of Economics and Statistics* **56**(4), 437–449.

Robinson, E. (2013). Chinese cotton policy: Social stability, not trade. Retrieved from: http://deltafarmpress.com/cotton/chinese-cotton-policy-social-stability-not-trade.

Rodrik, D. (1995). Political economy of trade policy. In G. M. Grossman and K. Rogoff (Eds.), *Handbook of International Economics* (pp. 1457–1494). North Holland: Elsevier Science Ltd.

Rozelle, S. and Swinnen, J. F. M. (2010). Agricultural distortions in the transition economies of Asia and Europe. In K. Anderson (Ed.), *The Political Economy of Agricultural Price Distortions*. Cambridge and New York: Cambridge University Press.

Political Risk Services (2013). *International Country Risk Guide*. Retrieved from: https://www.prsgroup.com/about-us/our-two-methodologies/icrg.

Shea, Y. P. (2003). *The Political Economy of China's Grain Policy Reform* (Ph.D.), The University of Adelaide, Adelaide, Australia. (PP42306).

Sheng, B. (2006). Political economy of China's trade policy: The evidence from industrial protection in 1990s. *Frontiers of Economics in China* **1**(3), 406–432.

Sims, C. A. (1980). Macroeconomics and reality. *Econometrica* **48**(10), 1–48.

Stigler, G. J. (1971). The theory of economic regulation. *The Bell Journal of Economics and Management Science* **2**(1), 3–21.

Stigler, G. J. (1975). *The Citizen and the State: Essays on Regulation.* Chicago: University of Chicago Press.

Swinnen, J. F. M. (1994). A positive theory of agricultural protection. *American Journal of Agricultural Economics* **76**(1), 1–14.

Swinnen, J. F. M. (2010a). Agricultural protection growth in Europe, 1870–1969. In K. Anderson (Ed.), *The Political Economy of Agricultural Price Distortions.* Cambridge and New York: Cambridge University Press.

Swinnen, J. F. M. (2010b). Political economy of agricultural distortions: The literature to date. In K. Anderson (Ed.), *The Political Economy of Agricultural Price Distortions.* Cambridge and New York: Cambridge University Press.

Swinnen, H. F. M. and Gorter, H. (1993). Why small groups and low income sectors obtain subsidies: The "altruistic" side of a "self-interested" government. *Economics and Politics* **5**(3), 285–293.

Swinnen, J. F. M., de Gorter, H., Rausser, G. C. and Banerjee, A. N. (2000). The political economy of public research investment and commodity policies in agriculture: An empirical study. *Agricultural Economics* **22**(2), 111–122.

The Cotton Outlook (2015). The cotlook A index plus: An explanation. (2014). Retrieved from https://www.cotlook.com/information/the-cotlook-a-index-plus-an-explanation/.

The sixth census of Chinese government and reports of the local government. (2014). Retrieved from: http://tieba.baidu.com/p/3622083537.

Thennakoon, J. (2015). Political economy of altering trade restrictions in response to commodity price spikes. *Review of Development Economics* **19**(2), 434–447.

Thennakoon, J. and Anderson, K. (2015). Could the proposed WTO special safeguard mechanism protect farmers from low international prices? *Food Policy* **50**, 106–113.

Tovar, P. (2009). The effects of loss aversion on trade policy: Theory and evidence. *Journal of International Economics* **78**(1), 154–167.

Tschirley, D. L. and Jayne, T. S. (2010). Exploring the logic behind southern Africa's food crises. *World Development* **38**(1), 76–87.

USDA (2015). Foreign Agriculture Service. Retrieved from: http://www.fas.usda.gov/.

Wang, X., Maeda, K., Hokazono, S. and Kaiser, H. M. (2014). Measuring the effects of a sliding scale duty system on China's cotton market: A spatial equilibrium approach. *Agribusiness* **30**(3), 345–365.

Wiggins, S. and Keats, S. (2009). *Grain Stocks and Price Spikes*. London: Overseas Development Institute.

World Bank (2012). *World Development Indicators 2012*, Washington DC. Retrieved from: http://data.worldbank.org/data-catalog/world-development-indicators.

World Bank (2016). *World Development Indicators 2016*. Washington DC. Retrieved from: http://data.worldbank.org/data-catalog/world-development-indicators.

Wright, B. (2002). Storage and price stabilization. In B. Gardner and G. Rausser (Eds.), *Handbook of Agricultural Economics* (Vol. 1): Elsevier Science B.V.

Wright, B. D. (2011). The economics of grain price volatility. *Applied Economic Perspectives and Policy* **33**(1), 32–58.

Wright, B. D. and Williams, J. C. (1982). The economic role of commodity storage. *The Economic Journal* **92**(367), 596–614.

Wright, B. D. and Williams, J. C. (1988). The incidence of market-stabilising price support schemes. *The Economic Journal* **98**(393), 1183–1198.

Zhai, F. and Hertel, T. W. (2010). China. In K. Anderson, J. Cockburn and W. Martin (Eds.), *Agricultural Price Distortions, Inequality, and Poverty*. Washington DC: The World Bank.

Zhang, X., Yang, J. and Wang, S. (2011). China has reached the Lewis turning point. *China Economic Review* **22**, 542–554.

Index

CPSIA information can be obtained
at www.ICGtesting.com
Printed in the USA
BVHW040726250920
589325BV00017B/16